What Readers Are Saying About *Live Inspired*

"In *Live Inspired*, Shirley masterfully weaves together stories from her life with the biblical narrative in such a way that, as a reader, you are drawn in. She is funny, relatable, and authentic all at once. *Live Inspired* helped me grasp grace in a way that my achievement-driven nature wouldn't always allow."

—Benjamin Hutchins, MRE,
Pastor of New River Valley Church, Blacksburg, VA

"Shirley's words and raw vulnerability took me through an engaging and enlightening journey in better understanding what it looks like to whole heartedly pursue overcoming performancism. Even after knowing Shirley for a couple years, this book gave me deeper insight into the brilliant, God-fearing woman that she is. If you're looking for a book filled with inspiring scriptures, personal real-life examples, and stories of people from the Bible brought to life, this is the one for you!"

—Natalie Gregory, Campus Ministry Leader,
Greater Pittsburgh Church of Christ, Pittsburgh, PA

"Vulnerable. Practical. Biblical. This is the book we didn't know we needed. Shirley invites the reader into her own journey through an often-underplayed topic and maps out a journey from misguided drive to the empowered life God intended."

—Jon and Lindsay Landis, Evangelist and Women's Ministry Leader, Roanoke Valley
Church, Roanoke, VA

"Shirley takes the reader with her by the hand on an active and progressive journey from the awareness of our self-driven tendencies—and their underlying cost—to the free and more enjoyable life meant by God. Very well documented with research and a thorough analysis of the Scriptures, this didactic book is also punctuated by numerous highly personal stories we can deeply relate to. This remarkable combination makes us willing to embark wholeheartedly on this transforming adventure—head, heart and soul."

—Armelle Neboit, Chief accountant at Nestlé and Author of "Job de Cœur", a blog
dedicated to Christians in the workplace

"Live Inspired offers realistic biblical truths to search as you work on living a spirit-led life. These biblical truths are helpful as you work on practical ways to overcoming the self-driven life, to living spirit filled. I really enjoyed Shirley's honesty along with her struggles on how God works in our lives daily, encouraging us to grow stronger in Him. In reading her book I am continually encouraged that God wants us to Live Inspired."

—Teresa Linner, Retired Elementary School Teacher, Pahrump, NV

"Shirley Desmond Jackson's book, *Live Inspired: Freeing Ourselves from the Grip of Performancism*, is a breath of fresh air for all of us overachievers and perfectionists. It's a comforting hug of understanding yet a challenging call to grow into grace."

—Eni Szabad, Student at Radford University, Radford, VA

"In *Live Inspired*, Shirley has creatively and accurately captured the nature of being driven by performancism. At times, it felt like she looked into our hearts and minds and expressed what has often been an ambiguous enigma of feelings and thoughts. This book is a must read for all of us who have ever struggled with the feelings of paralyzing fear of failure and finding self-worth in the rigid and merciless system of results only oriented thinking. This work has given us a vocabulary and framework to use to aid in our own journeys of growth and living a Spirit-led, inspired life."

—Delano and Nadine Stewart, Evangelist and Women's Leader, Valley Christian Las Vegas, NV

"I have enthusiastically believed in this book from its first edition to this newly expanded version. *Live Inspired: Freeing Ourselves from the Grip of Performancism* clearly and concisely walks with readers in the direction of freedom. The unexpected treasure to unearth in this book is the richness of a deeper relationship with God along with the added blessing of learning and being encouraged to rely more on the Holy Spirit. The encouragement to practice active memorization of scripture and times of silence and solitude is incredibly valuable for daily living. With deep insight, raw vulnerability, and biblical truths to bolster each chapter, the goal of becoming stronger in the Spirit began to enrich my life from the first chapter to the finish. This superb book is a gift to all readers who wish to live inspired through the love and grace of Jesus Christ."

—Jody Rohleder, Administrative Accountant RE/MAX Northwest, Westminster, CO

Live Inspired

Freeing Ourselves from the Grip of Performancism

Shirley Desmond Jackson

Live Inspired: Freeing Ourselves from the Grip of Performancism, Bible Study Companion
© Copyright 2024 Shirley Desmond Jackson

Published by Market Refined Publishing,
An Imprint of Market Refined Media, LLC
193 Cleo Circle
Ringgold GA 30736
marketrefinedmedia.com

Print ISBN: 979-8-9903602-8-0
Digital ISBN: 979-8-9903602-9-7
Library of Congress Control Number: 2024920008

Cover and Interior Design by Nelly Murariu at PixBeeDesigns.com
Manuscript Edits by Market Refined Media, LLC

Printed in the United States of America

First Edition: October 2024

How To Use This Bible Study Companion

Welcome to the next step in your living inspired journey! This Bible Study is meant to be a companion to the book, *Live Inspired: Freeing Ourselves from the Grip of Performancism.*

The book was written to inform you of your self-driven nature and how it leads to performancism. This Bible study is designed to take you further in your journey by bridging the gap between what you *know* and what you *do.* Immersing yourself in the material will deepen your heart's connection to God's truths so the Holy Spirit can bring His transformative power into your life.

I'm excited for you to dive deep into God's Word and begin experiencing the power of the Spirit-led life!

Each chapter is set up to follow a six-day schedule and each day's study should take an average of twenty to thirty minutes. All the chapters, except for chapter three, follow this pattern:

Day One: Introduction

This day starts by reviewing content from the book. There is a short narrative to reintroduce the topic. This is followed by an opening question to help us set the stage for the study.

Day Two: Read and Note

This is the first day of Bible study. In this section, we will read a passage together and pull information from the text.

Day Three: Reflect and Apply

As we reflect on the passage from the day before, we will look for the princi-ples they present. In the process, we will apply them to our current situation.

Day Four: Read and Note

We will continue reading a text and pulling information from it.

Day Five: Reflect and Apply

As we reflect on the passage from the day before, we will look for the prin-ciples they present. In the process, we will continue to apply them to our current situation.

Day Six: Resolve to Take Action

On this day we will wrap up our study for the week. As we do, we will resolve to take action to apply what we have learned.

Chapter Three is a uniquely formatted Bible study. It is still divided into six parts, however they don't follow the same pattern as the others.

Although each chapter is set up to be completed in six days, this is only a suggestion. Some people will naturally read more slowly or more quickly. It's more important for you to take your time. Allow the scriptures and prin-ciples to seep into your heart and mind.

You may read the verses from your favorite version of the Bible. I encourage you to also read them in a few different translations so you can get a fuller understanding. Whenever possible, do the study with a few friends. I've found this can be more enjoyable and lead to a richer learning experience.

As you work through this study, know that my heart and prayers are with you. May the Holy Spirit lead you to the Spirit-led life!

Table of Contents

Chapter 1: Seeking Spirit-Led Truths   1

Chapter 2: Grasping Grace   21

Chapter 3: Favoring Failure   37

Chapter 4: Sifting Success   53

Chapter 5: Aligning Allegiance   73

Chapter 6: Building Boundaries   93

Chapter 7: Easing Expectations   111

Chapter 8: Cultivating Collaboration   125

Chapter 9: Letting The Spirit Lead   141

Acknowledgments   157

About the Author   160

Endnotes   161

Notes   163

CHAPTER 1

Seeking Spirit-Led *Truths*

Day One: Introduction

This week we will look more closely at how Satan sows his lies into our hearts and how we can exchange those lies for God's truths. As we start, take a moment to read or review the information covered in chapter one of the book.

The Lie: "Good enough" is never good enough.

"I wish I could find my *good enough* button," my carpool partner fumed. Sighing, I nodded in agreement. My colleague's comment didn't express a genuine desire to find a reasonable standard for her work. Rather, her words expressed scathing criticism of our coworkers.

Due to extreme budget cuts, we had been reassigned to an elementary school about fifty miles outside our hometown. We loved our students who approached their lessons with refreshing enthusiasm. Yet despite all our efforts, their scores on standardized tests consistently fell below an acceptable range.

These students faced unique challenges. Their families didn't speak English and lived in a tight-knit community where it wasn't needed. So, their only exposure to English was in the classroom. While their parents respected teachers as authority figures, they didn't seek higher education as a goal for their children. Our coworkers believed these challenges justified accepting substandard scores as a part of life.

My colleague and I couldn't agree with this point of view. Our students' "failure" meant we failed. So, we doubled our efforts in hopes of finding the magic formula to their success. We felt disdain for our peers who had settled. From our perspective, "good enough" meant mediocre. So, imagine my surprise when I recently learned the term "good enough" actually means *adequately good for the circumstances*[1].

I'm not sure when I began to equate "good enough" with failure. But by the time I accepted that teaching assignment, this conviction had become deeply ingrained in my heart. "Good enough" implied falling short of excellent, so I always pushed myself to achieve a little more.

As self-driven achievers, it's easy for us to get caught up in wanting more. In what areas of your life is "good enough" never truly *good enough*?

....

....

....

....

....

....

....

....

....

Day Two: Exchanging the Truth for a Lie—Eve

It may surprise you, as it did me, that doubting the validity of "good enough" has its roots in the first lie recorded in the Bible. Let's look at how Satan planted it into the heart of the very first woman, Eve.

✎ Read and Note

Read Genesis 1:27–31.

Let's look closely at this first picture of Adam and Eve. As you read the passage, outline some truths about their creation. Specifically, in whose image were they created? What responsibilities were they given and what resources did they have? Did they lack anything they needed to fulfill these responsibilities?

_____

_____

_____

_____

_____

_____

_____

_____

_____

On the sixth day, God looked out at His finished creation which included Adam and Eve. What words did He use to describe it? How does this relate to the phrase "good enough?"

Let's look a little deeper at the creation of Eve. Read Genesis 2:18–22. What prompted God to create her?

_____

_____

_____

_____

_____

From Genesis 1 we know Eve was created in the image of God and that He described His creation as "very good." But now we see a new detail. The Hebrew verb translated as "made" in verse 22 is *banah*. It can also be translated as built or fashioned.[2] In English, the verb *to fashion* means to give a custom shape or to accommodate or adapt.[3] What does this tell you about how God created Eve? Did she lack anything?

_____

_____

_____

_____

_____

_____

As we move forward, keep in mind these truths about how God created Eve. Let's turn now to the entrance of the first lie. Read Genesis 3:1–8.

We see Satan enter the scene in the form of a serpent. As he begins his conversation with Eve, what truth does she understand about God's plan for her and Adam?

....

....

....

....

....

....

What tactic does Satan use to shake Eve's conviction of what is true? Who and what does he cause her to doubt?

....

....

....

....

....

....

....

If we look ahead to Genesis 3:19, God tells Adam and Eve they came from dust and to dust they will return. In other words, they will now experience physical death as one of the consequences of their disobedience. Look carefully at verses 3–4. What did Eve understand would happen if she ate, or even touched, the fruit from this tree? What bald-faced lie did Satan tell her?

....

....

....

....

....

....

But Satan also told her another lie, one which is far more subtle. Reread verse 5. Even though she had been created in God's image, Satan convinced her that "very good" wasn't "good enough." What lie did Eve *now* believe? What did she suddenly decide she lacked?

....

....

....

....

....

....

When Eve believes the lie that she needs something more, she eats from the tree and encourages Adam to do the same. Reread verse 7. What do Adam and Eve do after they eat from the tree? Why do you think they suddenly felt the need to do this?

....

....

....

....

....

Reread verse 8. What did Adam and Eve do after they made coverings for themselves? What does this reveal about their relationship with God?

....

....

....

....

....

....

....

Day Three: Exchanging the Truth for a Lie—Eve

💬 Reflect and Apply

For many years when I read Eve's story, I struggled to understand how she could be so easily deceived. But that was because I failed to see the parallels between her story and mine. Let's look at some ways we can relate to Eve's story.

Like her, God created each of us with a plan and a purpose.

> "For we are God's handiwork, created in Christ Jesus to do good works, which God prepared in advance for us to do."
>
> Ephesians 2:10

The Greek word translated as "handiwork," *poiéma*, can also be defined as workmanship, which has the connotation of *craftsmanship*[4]. God didn't just make us adequately good. He *perfectly crafted* us for the work He means for us to do.

What are some of the responsibilities God has given you? In what ways does He perfectly equip you for these works?

Like Eve, we can doubt God's plan and provision and fall for the lie that we need something more. As a self-driven achiever, I tried to compensate for what I lacked by working hard and building a resume of accomplishments.

In what ways have you doubted God and tried to overcompensate for what you thought you lacked?

....

....

....

....

When we exchange God's truth for the lie, we suddenly see all the ways we are not enough. And like Eve, we feel the need to make a cover for ourselves. For me, this meant putting masks over my doubts, fears, insecurities, and weaknesses. I hoped each accomplishment would make me feel better, but instead, I always found myself reaching for the next achievement.

How do you try to cover up your perceived weaknesses and inadequacies?

....

....

....

....

As Eve's story concludes, we see a beautiful image of God's grace. Read Genesis 3:21. What does God do for Adam and Eve? In what ways might the coverings they created for themselves been inadequate?

....

....

....

....

Look up Galatians 3:26–27. How does God provide covering for your flaws and imperfections? How does this free you from the lie that you need something more than what God has already provided?

_____

_____

_____

_____

_____

_____

_____

_____

_____

_____

_____

_____

_____

_____

_____

_____

Day Four: Exchanging a Lie for the Truth—the Apostle Paul

The first person who comes to mind when I think of a self-driven achiever is the apostle Paul. Although he became an incredibly influential leader in the first church, he wasn't one of the original twelve apostles. His conversion came later. Let's look at his story in more detail.

✎ Read and Note

Even before he became a Christian, Paul had already built an impressive resume of achievements. We'll begin our study of Paul by looking at a passage that describes his life before he met Jesus.

Read Philippians 3:3–6.

As you read the passage, make a list of what Paul achieved prior to becoming a Christian.

_____

_____

_____

_____

_____

_____

According to the Jewish standards of his time, Paul's ancestry and education were flawless. His family hailed from the respected tribe of Benjamin and raised him in accordance with the strict traditions of their faith.[5] His ability to speak both Aramaic and Hebrew (Hebrew of Hebrews), distinguished him from the Jews who only spoke Greek.[6] His efforts earned him a place in the elite religious party of the Pharisees. As experts of the law, they strove to please God through their diligent obedience. They especially fought against any ideology or person that threatened the purity of Judaism. When Paul claimed he achieved faultless righteousness based on the law, he didn't mean perfection. But he did achieve the standard of righteousness of his time.[7]

Let's turn now to look at the first time we are introduced to Paul. As you read the passage, remember what you know of his religious training and accomplishments. (Keep in mind that Saul was Paul's name in Hebrew.)

Read Acts 8:1–3.

These verses immediately follow the stoning of Stephen, the first Christian martyr. What picture do you now have of Paul?

....

....

....

....

Look back at what Paul said of himself in Philippians 3:6. What word did he use to describe his drive and actions for God?

....

....

....

....

....

You may wonder how a zealous man who loved God could justify his actions. Look at what Jesus said to His disciples in John 16:2–3. What lie fueled Paul's drive?

....

....

....

....

Let's continue studying Paul's life. His full conversion story is found in Acts 9:1–22. For the purposes of our study, we will break it down into smaller parts.

Read Acts 9:1–6 and describe what happened to Paul.

....

....

....

....

On the road to Damascus, Paul didn't just learn the truth; he met Jesus who is *the Truth* (John 14:6). All his life Paul had been zealous for his God. This included persecuting disciples because they represented a threat to Judaism. What truth did he now face? What lie did it contradict?

....

....

....

....

Let's continue by reading Acts 9:8–9. What happened to Paul after he met Jesus? What did he do to seek the help of the Holy Spirit?

....

....

....

....

When Paul faced the truth about Jesus, he experienced what we call *cognitive dissonance*. This is the uncomfortable feeling of recognizing two opposing points of view. Suddenly Paul had a choice. He could continue to believe the lie, or he could exchange it for the truth.

Look ahead to Acts 9:17–22. What decision did Paul make about Jesus?

....

....

....

....

What did Paul immediately begin to do after his conversion? How did he channel his zeal for God? What was the reaction of the people?

....

....

....

....

As we close out our study on Paul's life, let's continue reading where we left off in Philippians.

Read Philippians 3:7–9. How did Paul feel about his accomplishments after he met Jesus? What is the new source of his righteousness?

Day Five: Exchanging a Lie for the Truth—the Apostle Paul

💬 Reflect and Apply

Look back at the characteristics of a self-driven achiever in chapter one of the book. Which of these characteristics describes your life?

....

....

....

....

Until he met Jesus, Paul blindly followed a lie. Think about the self-driven characteristics you listed above. Each is rooted in a lie from Satan. How have you blindly followed these lies (i.e., how ingrained in your character are these traits)?

....

....

....

....

After Paul met Jesus on the road to Damascus, he suffered physical blindness for three days. How have you suffered from the lies you believed?

....

....

....

....

Paul embraced the truth and immediately began preaching that Jesus is the Son of God (Acts 9:20). How can your life change after you embrace the truth? (Refer to the characteristics of the Spirit-led achiever in chapter one of the book.)

_____

_____

_____

_____

_____

_____

Paul embraced the truth with the same zeal he did the lie. How can you imitate his example as you seek Spirit-led truths?

_____

_____

_____

_____

_____

_____

_____

Day Six: Conclusion

Truth: God's Word is Truth

Spirit-Led Conviction: I will exchange Satan's lies for God's truths.

⊙ Resolve to Take Action

As we wrap up our study on *Seeking Spirit-Led Truths*, spend some time with the Holy Spirit. Ask Him to reveal your answers to the following questions:

Look at the list of Spirit-led characteristics in chapter one of the book. How different would your life look if these characteristics became part of who you are?

....

....

....

....

....

....

....

....

When we renounce Satan's lies, and embrace God's truths, it changes how we live. As we read through the book of Acts, we see that Paul faced distrust from the disciples and rejection from the Jewish leaders. Yet despite the opposition, he continued to pursue the truth.

What opposition do you anticipate you will face as you let go of your self-driven characteristics and replace them with God's truths? What will help you stay motivated?

....

....

....

....

....

As you conclude your time with the Holy Spirit, write out a statement of commitment. Here are some examples:

- I will faithfully apply the Biblical principles I learn so I can move from a self-driven achiever to a Spirit-led achiever.

- I will learn to rest in the security of God's unconditional love and trust in His truths.

....

....

....

....

....

....

....

Write out a prayer to God. Share with Him your commitment to trust His truths and ask Him to help you.

....

....

....

....

....

....

....

....

....

....

....

....

....

....

CHAPTER 2

Grasping Grace

Day One: Introduction

In our study this week, we will build a true understanding of God's grace and how it impacts our self-worth and confidence. Before we begin, please take the time to read or review the information from chapter two in the book.

The Lie: I am only worth what I can produce.

Self-Driven Stronghold: I will build my self-worth and self-confidence through my achievements.

My heart beating wildly in my chest, I opened my door and stepped into the street. My bewildered eyes took in the car sitting by the side of the road. The driver's side mirror hung by a few wires and the door had a new dent. There could be no mistake. A corresponding dent on my back bumper clearly proved I had caused the damage.

Shaking, I made my way to the front door of the house which stood behind the parked car. After confessing and apologizing for what I had done, the owners followed me to the street so I could give them my insurance information.

I expected them to be angry, or at least frustrated; I deserved nothing else. Not only did they express forgiveness, but they also treated me with incredible kindness and compassion. After we finished filing the insurance claim, they gave me a bottle of water and expressed concern for my well-being. Suddenly the tears I had been suppressing all night began to trickle down my cheeks.

Kindness affects me like that. When I've done wrong, I anticipate and almost welcome some sort of punishment. Unexpected forgiveness and sympathy fill my heart with overwhelming and confusing emotions. I'm at a loss for words, and I'm not sure how to respond. It's the same reaction I have to God's grace.

At the root of my discomfort is a deeply held belief that I am, by nature, unworthy. I overcompensate for this by building my value and worth through my accomplishments.

As we explored in chapter two of *Live Inspired*, using achievements to compensate for feeling unworthy is a common characteristic of self-driven achievers. How do you respond to unmerited grace? What does your struggle reveal about your sense of feeling worthy?

....

....

....

....

....

....

....

....

....

....

....

....

Day Two: The Bleeding Woman's Affliction and Hope

One of Satan's most powerful lies attacks our very core. He tells us that in our natural state, we are unworthy. Let's look at how he used this lie to torment a woman in the New Testament. We never learn her name, but this woman's story appears in three of the Gospels. We will focus on the account in the Gospel of Mark.

✎ Read and Note

Read Mark 5:21–28.

The bleeding woman's story takes place in Capernaum, a small fishing town located on the north shore of the Sea of Galilee. Earlier, Jesus had preached throughout Galilee and healed many people. Because of this, great crowds followed Him everywhere. People suffering from all types of afflictions came to Him for healing.

From verses 21–24, describe the setting for the woman's story. Who else is there? What is the pressing concern?

....

....

....

....

....

....

....

....

How does Jesus respond? What does this tell us about Him?

....

....

....

....

....

Now that we know the setting, let's look at the entrance of the woman by rereading verses 25–26.

Try to imagine this woman's situation. What problem did she face?

....

....

....

....

....

Because of her physical affliction, she is often referred to as "the bleeding woman." Based on the Greek wording, many scholars believe she suffered from menorrhagia or excessive menstrual discharge.[1] As such, her illness carried many social consequences.

During the days of their menstrual period, the law of Moses required Hebrew women to sequester themselves. People who touched a menstruating woman had to bathe, wash their clothes, and isolate until evening (Leviticus 15:19–30).

These laws may seem harsh to our Western worldview because we know to use gloves and other personal equipment to protect us from blood-borne diseases. But at that time, quarantine was the only way people knew to keep diseases from spreading.

This woman was isolated from other people for twelve years. How might she be feeling at this point?

....

....

....

....

In addition to the physical and social consequences of her illness, this woman faced spiritual ones as well. A common belief about illnesses is illustrated by the disciples in John 9:2. What did they believe had caused the man's blindness?

....

....

....

Think about this woman who not only endured social isolation for twelve years but also faced the scorn and disapproval of those who believed her affliction resulted from sin.

What did she do to try and find a cure? Was she successful?

....

....

....

The bleeding woman depleted all her resources, remained a social outcast, and still suffered physically. When you think of her situation, what adjectives would you use to describe her emotional well-being or state of mind?

....

....

....

Somehow, she heard about Jesus, and hope pushed her to try one more time. Look at verse 27. How did she approach Him? How did her approach differ from Jairus in verse 22? What does this tell you about her self-esteem?

....

....

....

Think about how many people she must have touched as she pressed into the crowd to reach Jesus. According to the law, what implications did her actions have for all those she touched, including Jesus?

....

....

....

Consider the risk this woman took. What motivated her to take it?

....

....

....

Day Three: The Bleeding Woman's Affliction and Hope

💬 Reflect and Apply

When I read the bleeding woman's story, my heart aches for her. I can see how the enemy has sown the ancient lie in her heart: *"I am not worthy."* After twelve years, she became convinced of it. From the sidelines, she watched others, whom she believed to be much more worthy than herself, live the full life she could never attain.

Even though we don't suffer from a bleeding disease, we can relate to this woman. Our performancism took root because we doubted our worth. How have your feelings of unworthiness distanced you from other people?

....

....

....

Has the stress of your self-driven performancism affected your physical health? In what ways?

....

....

....

Like the bleeding woman, we know the disillusionment created by unfulfilled hope. We anticipate our accomplishments will make us feel worthy. How has your life of achievement led to unfulfilled hope?

....

....

....

The bleeding woman didn't have enough confidence to approach Jesus face-to-face. Instead, she crept up from behind and tried to take just a little piece of His power.

In what ways does feeling unworthy affect the way you approach Jesus? How do you try to take just a *little piece* of His power? Why do you do this?

....

....

....

....

....

....

The bleeding woman's desperation and hope in Jesus pushed her to take a great risk. Think about the frustration of trying to build your self-worth and confidence through your achievements. How can Jesus give you hope?

....

....

....

....

....

....

Day Four: The Bleeding Woman's Healing and Freedom

Fortunately, the bleeding woman's story doesn't end at Mark 5:28. Let's continue to unwrap her story.

✎ Read and Note

Read Mark 5:29–34.

What happened after the woman touched Jesus' clothes?

....

....

....

Imagine how the woman felt when she realized she was free of her suffering. What emotions might she be feeling? Do you think she felt worthy of His healing?

....

....

....

Reread verses 30–32 to see what happens next. As you think about this crowd pressing against Jesus, imagine a shopping mall during the holidays. What emotions do the disciples express?

....

....

....

Why do you think Jesus insisted on finding the woman?

Look at how the woman responds to Jesus in verse 33. Why do you think she felt afraid? What does it say about her feelings of self-worth?

Jesus gave the woman a title in verse 34. What was it?

Jesus healed many people and commended several people for their faith. But she is the only woman He ever called "Daughter." By calling her "Daughter," what truth did Jesus clarify about her identity and worth?

Review the last words Jesus spoke to the woman in verse 34. Do they surprise you?

Do you find it confusing for Jesus to tell the woman to have peace and to be free from her suffering? Wasn't she already freed of it? Why did He tell her to have peace? Let's look at what happens next to help us understand.

Read verses 35–36. What news did the people bring to Jesus? Who prevented Jesus from getting there on time? How might this information make the woman feel?

....

....

....

....

....

....

If I were this woman, I would feel like I had stolen my healing from Jairus' daughter. I can hear her thinking, "Certainly, the daughter of a synagogue ruler is more worthy of healing than me."

How would Jesus' words help the woman when she heard the news about his daughter? In the book, we talk about holy confidence—a confidence built on our relationship with God and His truths. How might His words give this to her?

....

....

....

....

....

....

Day Five: The Bleeding Woman's Healing and Freedom

💬 Reflect and Apply

The story of the bleeding woman has always moved my heart. Like her, we also became daughters of the King when we turned our lives over to Jesus. How does the title "Daughter" clarify your identity and worth? How can this free you from trying to build your worth and identity through achievements?

....

....

....

....

....

....

The bleeding woman was also inadequate. She could not achieve healing with her own power. But she had confidence in the power of Jesus to heal her. As you think about your life, what limitations do you see? How can the power of Jesus bring you healing?

....

....

....

....

....

God made us His daughters through the sacrifice of Jesus. As our Father, He sees where we are inadequate and wants to meet our needs. How can these two truths help you build holy confidence?

....

....

....

....

Unlike the disciples, Jesus was willing to take the time to find the woman. He wanted to meet all her needs, even the ones she didn't voice or knew she had. How does this encourage you on your journey?

....

....

....

....

Jesus' last words to the woman confirmed her identity as a daughter and promised freedom from all her suffering (present and future). Think about how these truths apply to you. What hope do they give you? How can they give you holy confidence when Satan attacks your worth?

....

....

....

....

Day Six: Conclusion

Truth: God has set our value and identity through the sacrifice of His Son.

Spirit-Led Conviction: I will grasp God's grace and love as the determination of my identity and worth and stand with holy confidence.

⊘ Resolve to Take Action

As we wrap up our study of the bleeding woman, spend some time with the Holy Spirit. Ask Him to reveal your answers to the following questions:

Describe how different your life would look if you embraced your identity as God's daughter and accepted His valuation of your worth. How would holy confidence protect you from trying to earn your worth?

....

....

....

....

....

....

....

....

....

....

The bleeding woman took many steps to find healing and freedom. First, she put her hope in Jesus. Then she took a great risk to reach out to Him. She received Jesus' definition of her value and identity as a daughter of the King. Finally, she heard His call to be free from all her suffering.

Which of these steps do you need to take in your own journey toward healing and freedom? What could stand in your way?

....

....

....

....

Write out a personal goal or statement of commitment to help you in your journey. For example:

- I will focus on my identity as a daughter of the King by meditating on Mark 5:34.

- I will release my inadequacies to God so I can receive mercy in my time of need.

....

....

....

....

....

....

Write out a prayer to God. Share with Him your commitment to take the necessary steps toward your healing and freedom. Ask Him to help you embrace your identity and worth.

....

....

....

....

....

....

....

....

....

....

....

....

....

....

....

....

....

Favoring Failure

Day One: Introduction

In chapter three of the book, *Favoring Failure*, we examine the root of our fear of failure, and the strongholds we create to avoid it. We learned that we have another choice: We can learn to embrace the lessons failure can teach us. Please take a few minutes to read or review the information from that chapter. In this study, we will learn how to respond to failures with a growth mindset by examining the life of the apostle Peter.

The Lie: Failure is a final judgment that diminishes my value.

Self-Driven Stronghold: I will avoid failure at all costs.

Another great example of a disciple who learned to rise again after failure is the apostle Peter. Outspoken, brash, and impulsive, no one ever had to guess what he thought or felt. His candid nature and willingness to take risks earned him both praise and rebukes. Because of his refreshing transparency, we can learn so much about how to respond to the failures in our lives.

Peter's birth name was Simon. Every list of the apostles in the New Testament starts with Simon and includes a parenthetical note that he was also called Peter (Matthew 10:2–4, Mark 3:16–19, and Luke 6:14–16). Both Peter (Greek) and Cephas (Aramaic) mean rock. Jesus gave Peter this nickname early in their relationship (John 1:42). It would take several years, filled with successes and failures, before Peter grew into his nickname.

Jesus gave Peter his nickname based on his potential, not his present reality. What does this tell us about the nature of God? What type of mindset (growth or fixed) does He model for us?

....

....

....

Day Two: Key Events in the Life of the Apostle Peter

✎ Read and Note

I'd like us to look at some key events in the apostle Peter's life and draw conclusions about how he faced his failures. As we do so, I'd like you to indulge me by using your imagination and interacting with the content.

Each scene below highlights a different event in the life of Peter. Just like us, his life included a mixture of successes and failures. After you read through each scene, make notes of how you think Peter must have felt at the end of it. Using a scale from one to ten, where one equals depths of despair and ten equals top-of-the-world exuberance, chart his feelings in the graph below.

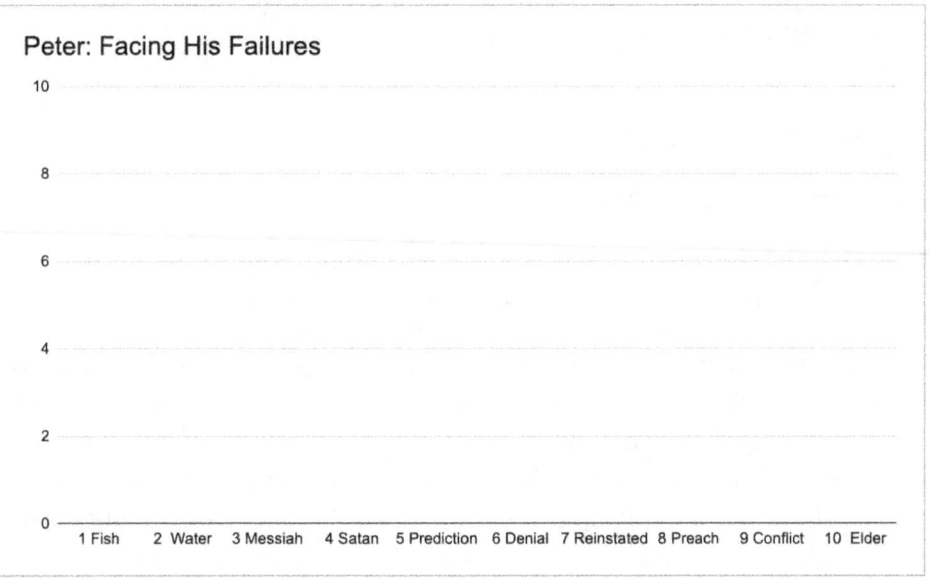

Peter: Facing His Failures

Scene 1: The Miraculous Catch of Fish

Full Text: Luke 5:1–11

Key Verse: "When Simon Peter saw this, he fell at Jesus' knees and said, 'Go away from me, Lord; I am a sinful man!'" Luke 5:8

Imagine the Scene: You have been fishing all night and caught nothing. You are tired and frustrated. The Messiah asks you for the use of your boat. You reluctantly agree and wait for Him to finish teaching. But instead of releasing you to rest, He advises you to try fishing once more.

Exasperated, you respond with sarcasm but still obey. The unexpected and enormous catch of fish unleashes conflicting emotions. You suddenly realize the sovereignty of Jesus, and the disrespectful way you spoke to him. Throwing yourself at His knees, you ask Him to go away. But He invites you to follow Him and gives you a new purpose instead.

Scene 2: Walking on Water

Full Text: Matthew 14:25–32

Key Verse: "Immediately Jesus reached out his hand and caught him. 'You of little faith,' he said, 'why did you doubt?'" Matthew 14:31

Imagine the Scene: You are one of the twelve chosen apostles. You have spent an amazing day with the Messiah, watching Him teach the crowds and witnessing the miracle of feeding the five thousand. You saw Him walk on water and answered the invitation to join Him. For a few steps, you feel the exhilaration of achieving the impossible. But then your doubts cause you to fall. Jesus rescues you, but He notes you have "little faith," and He wonders why you doubted.

Scene 3: Proclaiming Jesus as the Messiah

Full Text: Matthew 16:13–20

Key Verses: "Simon Peter answered, 'You are the Messiah, the Son of the living God.' Jesus replied, 'Blessed are you, Simon son of Jonah, for this was not revealed to you by flesh and blood, but by my Father in heaven.'" Matthew 16:16–17

Imagine the Scene: You have taken a chance and answered a question asked by the greatest teacher of all time. You've stepped out on faith and affirmed your belief in His deity. When Jesus praises you for your answer, He notes you have received a revelation from God. Then He gives you a unique responsibility. By calling you by your special nickname, He reaffirms His vision for you.

Day Three: Key Events in the Life of the Apostle Peter

 **Read and Note**

Scene 4: Rejecting God's Plan

Full Text: Matthew 16:21–23

Key Verse: "Jesus turned and said to Peter, 'Get behind me, Satan! You are a stumbling block to me; you do not have in mind the concerns of God, but merely human concerns.'" Matthew 16:23

Imagine the Scene: Just a few moments ago, you received praise for sharing your divine revelation and received the keys to the kingdom of heaven. Jesus even called attention to His vision for you by using your nickname.

Suddenly, Jesus reminds you of your role as a follower. He rebukes you for your earthly thinking, calls you by His enemy's name, and accuses you of being a stumbling block to Him.

Scene 5: Predicting His Struggle

Full Text: Luke 22:31–34

Key Verse: "Jesus answered, 'I tell you, Peter, before the rooster crows today, you will deny three times that you know me.'" Luke 22:34

Imagine the Scene: Your teacher and Messiah has just revealed the trials you will soon face. He predicts you will fail, but because He is so certain you will return, asks you to remember to strengthen the other disciples.

You are confident of your readiness to suffer and even die for Jesus, but He is just as confident you will deny even knowing Him.

Scene 6: Denying Jesus

Full Text: Luke 22:54–62

Key Verses: "The Lord turned and looked straight at Peter. Then Peter remembered the word the Lord had spoken to him: 'Before the rooster crows today, you will disown me three times.' And he went outside and wept bitterly." Luke 22:61–62

Imagine the Scene: Once you were praised for recognizing and proclaiming Jesus as the Messiah. But now you have done the opposite. You publicly deny knowing Him three times as you warm yourself by the fire. The rooster suddenly crows, and Jesus turns and looks directly at you. Weeping bitterly, you wonder how you could have let your fear trump your faith.

Scene 7: Reinstating His Role as an Apostle

Full Text: John 21:4–17

Key Verse: "The third time he said to him, 'Simon son of John, do you love me?' Peter was hurt because Jesus asked him the third time, 'Do you love me?' He said, 'Lord, you know all things; you know that I love you.' Jesus said, 'Feed my sheep.'" John 21:17

Imagine the Scene: As you make it to the shore, you notice Jesus has built a fire. Suddenly you are transported back to a time when you warmed yourself in front of a similar fire. Three times on that evening you denied knowing Jesus and the memory grieves you.

But in this meeting, Jesus doesn't ask you why you denied Him. Instead, He asks, "Do you love me more than these (the fish)?" But when He asks, He doesn't use your special nickname. When you affirm that you love Him, He asks you to take care of His sheep. Jesus asks you the question a second time and again you assure Jesus that you love Him. Once more Jesus calls you to take care of His sheep.

When Jesus asks you a third time, you break down and confess that Jesus knows everything, including that you love Him. Once more He calls you to take care of His sheep. After the third time you understand Jesus wants you to forget your past. Because He knows you love Him, He wants you to take care of His sheep.

Day Four: Key Events in the Life of the Apostle Peter

Scene 8: Preaching the First Gospel Message

Full Text: Acts 2:29–41

Key Verses: "With many other words he warned them; and he pleaded with them, 'Save yourselves from this corrupt generation.' Those who accepted His message were baptized, and about three thousand were added to their number that day." Acts 2:40–41

Imagine the Scene: You failed the Messiah, but He gives you another chance. After His resurrection, you preach the first Gospel message and see three thousand people come to faith.

Scene 9: Conflict with the Apostle Paul

Full Text: Galatians 2:11–14; 2 Peter 3:15

Key Verse: "When I [Paul] saw that they were not acting in line with the truth of the gospel, I said to Cephas [Peter] in front of them all, 'You are a Jew, yet you live like a Gentile and not like a Jew. How is it, then, that you force Gentiles to follow Jewish customs?'" Galatians 2:14

Imagine the Scene: You have been an instrumental figure in the early church. Your voice and testimony convince others that God opened the door of salvation to the Gentiles (Acts 11:15–18). But when a powerful group of Jewish disciples begins to insist Gentiles need to be circumcised before becoming Christians, you become afraid of offending them. You stop eating with the Gentile believers in observance of the Old Testament law. Other disciples follow you in your hypocrisy.

When the apostle Paul sees this, he corrects you for it. Recognizing he speaks the truth, you repent. Later, you write of Paul as a dear brother who speaks with the wisdom of God.

Scene 10: Serving as an Elder of the Church

Full Text: 1 Peter 5:1–4

Key Verse: "To the elders among you, I appeal as a fellow elder and a witness of Christ's sufferings who also will share in the glory to be revealed." 1 Peter 5:1

Imagine the Scene: You have faithfully served the Lord as a preacher and an elder. You have shepherded the Lord's people and are now instructing others to do the same. You are looking forward to receiving the crown of glory that will never fade.

Day Five: Analyzing The Results

💬 Reflect and Apply

Take a moment to connect the points on your graph and reflect on the results. You can see my responses on the solid line of the following graph.

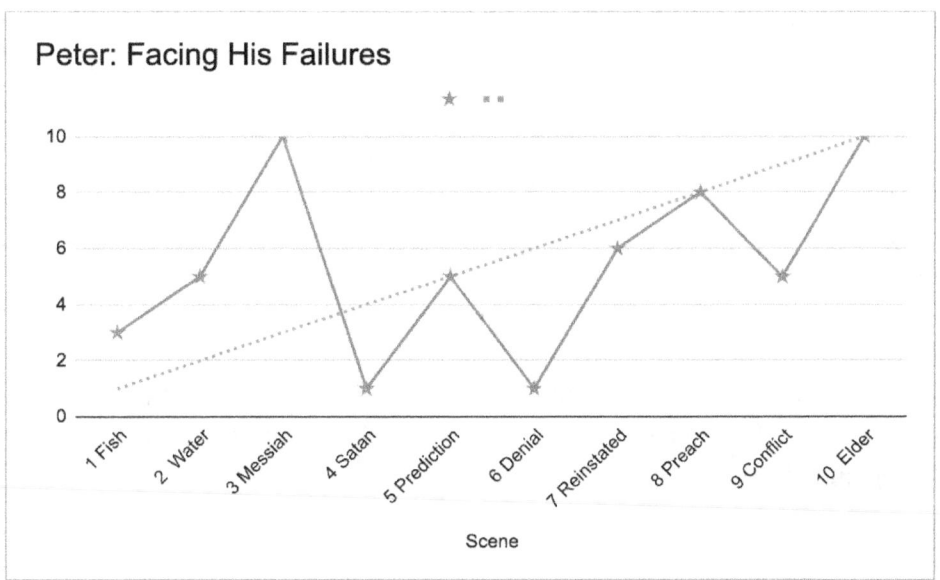

Depending on our individual emotional makeups, the peaks and valleys on our graphs may be higher or shorter, but the lines will follow the same pattern.

The dotted line in the graph above illustrates a steady, linear growth from the first event to the last. How does Peter's growth (on either your graph or mine) compare to the dotted line in the graph above? What does this teach us about the nature of growth?

....

....

....

Peter's growth line is marked with points of soaring success intermingled with points of falling failures. How would his graph look if he had stopped trying? Is there a point in his life where you would have been tempted to quit?

....

....

....

....

....

....

In the end, Peter's growth line ends up in the same place as if he had experienced a steady, linear growth. What does this tell us about Peter and his failures? Did they help or hinder him from maturing in the Lord? How does this principle apply to you?

....

....

....

....

....

....

....

When I think about how Peter felt after each scene, I see a myriad of emotions. But I never see him afraid to try again. Peter faced his failures, matured through his mistakes, and held on to hope. In what ways can you follow his example?

....

....

....

....

....

Peter consistently showed a growth mindset as he faced his failures. In what ways do you need to cultivate a growth mindset as you think about your failures?

....

....

....

....

....

....

....

Day Six: Conclusion

Truth: God allows failure to help us to grow.

Spirit-Led Conviction: I will favor failure as an essential part of the learning process.

⊘ Resolve to Take Action

When we release our stronghold of avoiding failure, we will allow it to be our teacher. Like Peter, facing our failures with a growth mindset will lead us to maturity. Someday when we track the events of our lives, we will see the same upward incline, dotted with our successes and failures.

As we conclude our study on Peter's journey of growth, take time to sit with the Holy Spirit. Ask Him to help you answer the following questions:

Describe how different your life would look if you allowed failure to be your teacher. How would it reduce your anxiety? Increase your willingness to take risks? How could it lead you to maturity?

....

....

....

....

What could prevent you from having a growth mindset toward failure? How will you overcome these obstacles?

....

....

....

From your time with the Holy Spirit, write out a personal goal or statement. For example:

- I will learn how to face failure with a growth mindset.

- I will remember the only true failure is not trying.

....

....

....

....

....

....

Write out a prayer to God. Share your determination to cultivate a growth mindset and ask Him to help you.

....

....

....

....

....

....

CHAPTER 4

Sifting Success

Day One: Introduction

In chapter four of the book, we examined the many ways the world influences our definitions and measurements of success. Please take a few minutes to read or review the information from the chapter. In this study, we will explore in more detail how God views and measures success by looking at the Parable of the Ten Minas.

The Lie: Only the end result matters.

Self-Driven Stronghold: I will be successful by focusing solely on my goal.

I watched as my fellow student began passing out the pop quiz. Starting with the front row, he moved slowly and double-checked the pages he gave to each student. Once students received their papers, they immediately began answering the questions. Within a few minutes the instructor asked us to put our pencils down.

Those of us, like me, who sat in the back of the room had a disadvantage. Unlike those who sat in the front, we only had time to answer the first half of the quiz. When the instructor asked us to share how many questions we answered correctly, I sat fuming in my seat. I could have been just as successful as my peers if I had been given the same amount of time.

Looking back, I realized my mistake. I'd fallen into the trap of measuring success solely by the end result. Instead of the overall total, I could have used a more accurate measurement to define my success. For example, I could have looked at the percentage of questions I answered correctly from the first half of the quiz.

As self-driven achievers, we strive to succeed because it ensures we won't fail. But as we saw in chapter four of the book, we tend to define success by the end result—and often our ability to achieve that result is compromised by either the situation or the actions of others.

How do you respond when your ability to succeed is compromised by people or circumstances beyond your control? How challenging is it for you to reframe your success with a more accurate measurement?

Day Two: The Nobleman Assigns Responsibilities

✎ Read and Note

Read Luke 19:11–14.

The primary purpose of this parable is to prepare the disciples for the impending departure of Jesus. Although He would soon leave this world, Jesus promised to return. The parable shows that Jesus expects His disciples to fulfill certain responsibilities during His absence. In this study, we will focus on the servants' assignments as well as their ability to complete them. As we do so, we will gain insight into God's view of success—which includes the journey and the outcome.

The story opens with a nobleman leaving for a foreign country to be crowned king. Jesus is describing a familiar scene to the people listening. Rome had a long-standing policy of establishing local rulers to govern Israel. Before beginning to rule, these noblemen had to travel to Rome and accept their appointment.[1]

Before he left, the nobleman called in ten of his servants. What responsibility did he give each of them?

....

....

....

....

....

....

....

The nobleman gave each servant one mina. What does this say about the fairness of the master?

....

....

....

....

....

....

....

How specific were the master's instructions? What does that say about his confidence in the servants and his commitment to a growth mindset?

....

....

....

....

....

....

....

At that time one mina equaled about three months' wages. When Jesus told this parable, few people had capital. Depending on their risk tolerance, those willing to lend money could potentially earn a return of five to ten times their original investment.[2]

The nobleman gave his servants full authority and freedom to carry out their responsibilities. What are some of the possible reactions the different servants might have had to this latitude?

....

....

....

....

....

....

Since each servant received the same resources and authority, would you expect them to have the same outcome? Why or why not?

....

....

....

....

....

....

....

....

Reread verse 14. What do we learn about the people's attitude toward the prospective ruler?

....

....

....

Because the Jewish people resented being under Roman rule, they would understand and sympathize with the people who opposed the appointment of the nobleman. How would their experience help them understand the contentious climate created by the nobleman's departure?

....

....

....

....

....

....

....

....

....

....

....

The servants would have to invest the nobleman's money in the community. Given the resistance of the other subjects, what challenges would they face on the journey to their goal? What might they learn by facing and overcoming these challenges?

....

....

....

....

In what ways would they have to leave their comfort zones? In what ways could this help them grow?

....

....

....

....

How could the servants define their success, so it includes both the journey and the end result?

....

....

....

....

....

Day Three: The Nobleman Assigns Responsibilities

💬 Reflect and Apply

The nobleman gave each servant what they needed for success. They each had the same amount of money and the freedom to invest it as they saw best. What has God given you to help you succeed in the important areas of your life?

....

....

....

....

....

....

How do you feel about the latitude God gives you to fulfill your responsibilities? Does it encourage you, challenge you, or intimidate you?

....

....

....

....

....

....

Think about how the servants had to manage the tension between their instructions and the resistance of those who didn't want to help their master. What types of resistance have you felt in your journey toward success? How can you reframe these challenges so they highlight what you learned? For example: *I grew in my conflict resolution skills.*

....

....

....

....

....

....

Each servant had to leave their comfort zone to invest the money. How strong is your risk tolerance? What causes you to shy away from trying something new? How can you reframe your fear of taking risks so you see the growth potential? For example: *I will grow in my risk tolerance by stepping out of my comfort zone.*

....

....

....

....

....

....

How can you change your definition of success so it includes the journey as well as the end result?

....

....

....

....

....

....

....

....

....

....

....

....

....

....

....

....

....

Day Four: The Nobleman Evaluates the Servants' Success

✎ Read and Note

Read Luke 19:15–26.

Despite the people's objections, the nobleman was made king and returned home. He promptly asked for an accounting from his servants.

Look at verses 16, 18, and 20 and the meetings he had with them. Why did he meet with each one individually? What would have happened if he discussed the servants' results in front of each other?

....

....

....

....

....

What does this reveal about the nobleman's respect for his servants?

....

....

....

....

....

Now look carefully at the results of each of the servants in verses 16, 18, and 20. They started with the same resource (one mina). How did their results differ?

What do the different returns reveal about each servant's risk tolerance?

Look at the reaction of the nobleman to the results of the first two servants in verses 17 and 19. What emotion does he express? Does he convey disappointment in the servant who earned less of a return?

What new assignments does the nobleman now give to the first two servants? How did he determine which assignment to give each of them?

....

....

....

....

How does the nobleman show a growth mindset for his servants?

....

....

....

Now let's look more closely at the third servant. Reread verses 20–21. What reason does the third servant give for not taking any risk? What accusation does he make about the nobleman?

....

....

....

....

How does the nobleman respond to these accusations in verses 22–23? How does he challenge the servant's false thinking?

....

....

....

....

....

....

....

What happens to the third servant in verses 24–26? Does he get a new assignment from the nobleman?

....

....

....

....

....

....

....

Day Five: The Nobleman Evaluates the Servants' Success

💬 Reflect and Apply

We live in a world where the comparison trap begins early and affects us all. In what ways do you struggle with comparing yourself to others?

....

....

....

....

....

When the nobleman kept the servants' results private, he protected them from the trap of comparison. What does this reveal about how God views your efforts and results?

....

....

....

....

....

....

The nobleman let his servants learn from their experiences. He adjusted their next responsibilities in keeping with their rate of growth. In what ways do you see God doing the same for you? How does this help you develop a growth mindset?

....

....

....

....

....

The third servant let his fear of failure keep him from taking any risks. Have you ever wondered why this servant falsely accused the nobleman? Maybe he believed the nobleman expected the same end result, even though each servant differed in abilities and risk tolerance. If so, the third servant could have felt like he had been set up to fail. Confident he couldn't succeed, he did nothing and blamed the nobleman for being unfair.

Have there been times when your success was measured solely by the outcome, even though you had fewer resources, training, or risk tolerance than your peers? How does an unfair situation affect your willingness to try?

....

....

....

....

....

Does the nobleman's decision to pull the mina away from the third servant seem harsh to you? Let's look at it through the lens of mindset. By refusing to take even the smallest and safest risk, the third servant chose to stay frozen in his fixed mindset. Without a willingness to try, no opportunity for growth, present or future, would benefit him.

What lesson can you learn from the third servant's refusal to try? Do you operate from a fixed or a growth mindset? What inspires you to adopt a growth mindset?

Day Six: Conclusion

Truth: Success needs to be measured by the journey as well as the end result.

Spirit-Led Conviction: I will sift my success by using fair and accurate measurements. The progress toward my goal is just as valuable as the end result.

⊘ Resolve to Take Action

As we've unpacked this parable, we see God desires for us to be successful. Because He understands our unique abilities, skills, and knowledge, God doesn't compare us to others. When we do the best with what God gives us, He accepts our efforts and helps us learn from our experiences. God's definition and measurement of success include both the journey and the final result.

Take some time to sit with the Holy Spirit as you consider the following questions:

Describe how different your life would look if you learned to enjoy your current journey and embraced the success God wishes you to have.

....

....

....

....

....

....

....

....

What keeps you from enjoying your current journey? How can a growth mindset help you reframe the challenges or setbacks you experience on it? For example: *My idea failed, but I learned what doesn't work.*

....

....

....

....

Write out a goal or statement of commitment to help you enjoy your current journey. For example:

- I will stop comparing myself to others and do my best with what God has given me.

- I will focus equally on the journey as I do the outcome.

....

....

....

....

Write out a prayer to God where you share your commitment to measure your success by both the journey and the end result. Ask Him to help you use fair measurements in your definition of success.

....

....

....

....

CHAPTER 5

Aligning Allegiance

Day One: Introduction

In chapter five of the book, we examined our people-pleasing tendencies and the snares they create. Aligning our allegiance to God frees us from those snares and sets us on the path of a Spirit-led life. Please take a few minutes to read or review the content from that chapter. In this study, we will examine how Jesus modeled both an allegiance to His Father as well as the traits of true likability.

The Lie: My ability to be successful depends on my popularity.

Self-Driven Stronghold: I will do whatever is necessary so people will like and accept me.

When I taught third grade, each of my students wrote and published their own book entitled, *When I'm 22.* The children wrote about what they thought their lives would look like when they entered the adult world. Their dream careers played a pivotal role in these books. I had several aspiring astronauts, teachers, nurses, stay-at-home moms, firefighters, and race-car drivers. While I loved reading their thoughts about these traditional career choices, the use of technology has changed the face of our workforce. As a public educator, I realized most of my students would choose careers that haven't even been discovered yet.

For example, today over half of the people born between 1996 and 2012 (Gen-Z) want to become social media influencers.[1] By definition, these influencers make money by promoting products and services on their social media accounts.[2] The more followers they have, the more money they could potentially make. In this profession, popularity drives success. The most successful influencers have a following of more than 1,000,000 people.[3]

If we look at the sheer number of followers, Jesus Christ is arguably the most influential person of all time. More than 2,000 years after His death, He still has more than two billion followers.[4] Yet Jesus didn't come to the Earth to simply become an incredible influencer. He came to fulfill God's purpose. His number of followers is a natural outgrowth of His life and ministry. While He didn't pursue popularity, He successfully changed this world forever.

What connection do you see between popularity and success? Do you feel it's necessary to please other people to be successful?

....

....

....

....

....

....

....

....

....

....

Day Two: Jesus Modeled Allegiance to His Father

As we saw in chapter five, we assume greater popularity leads to greater impact and success. Because of this, as self-driven achievers, we feel tempted to please other people to gain their approval or acceptance, even at the expense of our integrity or needs. But how did Jesus, the most influential person of all time, respond to the temptation to please others? We will look at how He responded to four different groups of people: the crowd who followed Him, the religious authorities, His family, and His friends.

✎ Read and Note

Let's look at how Jesus responded to the crowd by reading John 6:5–14.

The feeding of the five thousand is one of Jesus' most well-known miracles and it sets the scene for an important teaching. Because of the miraculous signs Jesus had performed, a great crowd of people began to follow Him. The scriptures only tell us how many men were in the crowd. We know from chapter five that scholars believe the true number, including women and children, was between 15,000 and 20,000.[5]

Reread verse 14. What does the crowd conclude after they witness this miracle?

....

....

....

....

....

....

After feeding the crowd, Jesus and His disciples went across the lake to Capernaum (John 6:15-21). When the crowd followed them there, Jesus challenged their motives.

Read John 6:26–27.

Why did the crowd follow Jesus? What did they hope to receive? How did Jesus respond to their motivation?

....

....

....

....

....

In the teaching that followed, Jesus reminded the people that God provided daily physical bread (*manna*) for the Israelites while they wandered in the desert (John 6:28–40). His pivotal point is found in verse 35. What claim does He make?

....

....

....

....

....

Jesus encouraged the people to seek spiritual blessings rather than physical ones. As the Bread of Life, Jesus promised to provide for their daily spiritual needs. To the Jewish people, Jesus' words would have sounded blasphemous.

Read John 6:60–66. How did the people react to this teaching? If Jesus wanted to please the crowd, how would He have responded to their objections?

....

....

....

....

....

....

....

....

Now let's look at how Jesus faced pressure from the religious leaders.

The Pharisees, the religious leaders of the time, enjoyed both prestige and power. Although they accepted the authority of the written Word of God, they gave equal weight to their oral tradition.[6] Jesus referred to these additional requirements as "heavy, cumbersome loads" (Matthew 23:4). Although Jesus always obeyed God's laws, He didn't succumb to the pressure of following the traditions of the Pharisees.

Read Luke 13:10–16.

In this passage, Jesus faced opposition from the synagogue ruler for healing a woman on the Sabbath—an act that violated the oral tradition but not the law of Moses.

How did Jesus respond to the criticism of the synagogue ruler? Did He apologize and agree to follow the oral tradition?

....

....

....

....

....

....

....

Read Matthew 12:9–14.

Jesus chose to heal this man on the Sabbath. How did the Pharisees respond to His continual refusal to submit to their oral tradition?

....

....

....

....

....

....

....

....

Let's turn our attention to how Jesus faced pressure from His family.

Read John 7:1–9.

Our families often have great influence on us. In this passage we learn that Jesus' brothers didn't believe in Him as the Messiah or understand His mission. They saw the Jewish Festival in Judea as an opportunity for Him to gain a larger following. So they advised Him to go to the Festival and to show Himself to the world.

How did Jesus respond to the pressure of His brothers? Did He accept their worldly advice?

....

....

....

....

Jesus' decision undoubtedly created tension with His brothers. But let's look ahead to a moment after His resurrection.

Read Acts 1:12–14.

All the believers are gathered together. Who is counted among them (verse 14)? Jesus trusted God, even when it created tension with His family. But this tension didn't prevent them from eventually becoming believers and followers of Jesus. How can this help us trust God if (or when) our families pressure us to compromise our faith?

....

....

....

....

Finally, let's look at the pressure Jesus faced from His friends.

Read John 12:1–8.

At a dinner given in honor of Jesus, Mary, the sister of Lazarus, anointed Him with an expensive perfume. Judas, one of Jesus' apostles and close friends, criticized her sacrifice. He reasoned that the perfume, valued at a year's salary, should have been sold and given to the poor.

How did Jesus respond to the criticism from Judas? Did He apologize for accepting the gift?

....

....

....

....

....

....

Read Mark 14:10–11.

What did Judas decide to do when he fell "out of like" with Jesus?

....

....

....

....

....

Day Three: Jesus Modeled Allegiance to His Father

💬 Reflect and Apply

We have looked at how the crowd, the religious leaders, as well as Jesus' family and friends resisted His plans and choices. From these examples, we know Jesus refused to seek affirmation, approval, or acceptance from people. He always aligned His allegiance with His Father:

> "So Jesus said, 'When you have lifted up the Son of Man, then you will know that I am he and that I do nothing on my own but speak just what the Father has taught me. The one who sent me is with me; he has not left me alone, for I always do what pleases him.'"
>
> John 8:28–29

In what ways do you find it difficult to resist peer pressure?

....

....

....

....

How do you find yourself wanting to please those who have authority over you?

....

....

....

....

Our family often has a special hold on us. In what ways do you find it difficult to resist the temptation to please them?

....

....

....

....

....

Our friends can exert great influence on us. How have you been tempted to give in to the pressure of friends?

....

....

....

....

....

Are you tempted to compromise your integrity to please someone or some people in your life? What do you fear will happen if you choose to please God instead?

....

....

....

....

....

Day Four: Jesus Modeled the Traits of Likability

We know Jesus chose to please His Father, rather than people. Because of this, people who did not honor God did not like Jesus. But that doesn't mean Jesus wasn't likable. In chapter five we saw how likability encompasses attributes such as making everyone feel heard, important, valued, and included. Let's look at how Jesus treated people who were typically overlooked and unappreciated in His culture.

✎ Read and Note

In most cultures, children have no status or power. In essence, they have no voice and represent the unheard members of their society.

Read Mark 10:13–16.

How do the disciples see the children in this passage? What was Jesus' perspective?

....

....

....

....

....

....

In the culture of this time, women did not have equal status with men. In religious assemblies, they sat segregated from men.[7] They could not own property or testify in court.[8] Jewish men spoke rarely to women and almost never in public.[9] As second-class citizens, they were seen as unimportant.

Read Luke 8:1–3.

This passage describes a time early in Jesus' ministry. As you read through this passage, who is included with His twelve disciples? What important role do they play?

....

....

....

....

Read Luke 10:38–39.

In their society, only men sat at the feet of a rabbi to learn from him.[10] But who is sitting at the feet of Jesus and listening to Him teach? What does this say about Jesus?

....

....

....

....

Read Matthew 28:1–10.

Who were the first ones to see Jesus after His resurrection? What responsibility did He give them?

....

....

....

....

Rabbis and religious leaders of Jesus' time did not associate with people who did not adhere to both the written law and oral tradition.[11] In their self-righteousness, they looked down on all sinners. But they especially despised the tax collectors because they corroborated with the Roman government and had a reputation for stealing from their Jewish peers. Because of their sins, these people were undervalued members of their society.

Read Matthew 9:9–13.

What was Matthew's profession before being called by Jesus? What is the significance of including him in His twelve apostles?

....

....

....

....

When Matthew hosted a dinner for Jesus, he invited his friends and colleagues. They are described as sinners and tax collectors which means they were notorious for their moral transgressions.

How did the Pharisees, the religious rulers, react when Jesus socialized with them? How does Jesus respond to their criticism? What does this say about Jesus?

....

....

....

....

....

Read Deuteronomy 7:6.

What does this passage say about the Israelites?

....

....

....

....

The Jewish people were very exclusive. They had been taught to separate themselves from the other cultures around them. The law commanded them to not intermarry with other people or to engage in their pagan worship (Deuteronomy 7:3–4). The law also gave specific instructions regarding diseases. Because of leprosy's contagious nature, leprous people had to live outside of the community (Leviticus 13:45–46).

God's law intended to create and protect His chosen people. Ultimately, He intended for His people to bless all peoples of the earth (Genesis 12:2–3). Unfortunately, the Jews had lost God's heart and looked at these people with antipathy. Gentiles (non-Jewish people), Samaritans (half-Jewish people), and lepers (those suffering from leprosy) were all marginalized.

Read Matthew 8:5–13.

The centurion was a Roman soldier (a Gentile) in charge of 100 men. Not only did Jesus heal his servant, but He gave the centurion an incredible compliment. What was it? How does this show the heart of Jesus?

....

....

....

....

Read Luke 10:30–37.

Jesus chose someone who was excluded from their society to be the hero of this parable. Who was it? By contrast, who are not heroes? What does this teach us about Jesus?

....

....

....

....

....

Read Mark 1:40–42.

Jesus chose to touch this man to heal him. Why is this significant? What does it say about the inclusive nature of Jesus?

....

....

....

....

....

....

Day Five: Jesus Modeled the Traits of Likability

💬 Reflect and Apply

In these examples, we see Jesus model the attributes of being likable.

He gave voice to the unheard people in his society (the children) and treated the unimportant people of His culture (the women) with respect. How can you listen to the concerns of people who are often overlooked?

....

....

....

....

....

Jesus included and cared for people who were notorious for their moral transgressions. How can you show the same love and care for people who don't yet follow Him?

....

....

....

....

....

He also valued and included people from all walks of life (lepers, Gentiles, and Samaritans). How can you show respect for people who don't have the same social status as you do?

....

....

....

....

Which of the attributes of being likable resonates the most with you?

....

....

....

....

....

Jesus focused on the needs of the other people and this made Him likable. How can you focus on becoming more likable rather than on being liked?

....

....

....

....

....

Day Six: Conclusion

Truth: True success depends on pleasing God rather than men.

Spirit-Led Conviction: I will align myself with Jesus. People will respond to me in the same ways as they did to Him.

Throughout His ministry, Jesus displayed the traits of likability. He showed no partiality and intended for His Gospel to include all people:

"And I, when I am lifted up from the earth, will draw all people to myself." John 12:32

⊘ Resolve to Take Action

As we conclude our study for this week, take some time to sit with the Holy Spirit. Ask Him to help you answer the following questions:

What would your life look like if you emulated Jesus' example of aligning allegiance to God and displaying the traits of likability? What would be different?

....

....

....

....

What opposition will you face as you imitate Jesus in these areas?

....

....

....

....

Write a statement of commitment to help you. For example:

- I will lean in and listen to the concerns of the people I supervise.

- I can live a life of confidence by staying anchored in the love and acceptance of God rather than seeking approval from people.

Write out a prayer to God where you pledge your allegiance to Him. Ask Him to help you cultivate the traits of likability as Jesus did.

CHAPTER 6

Building Boundaries

Day One: Introduction

In chapter six of the book, we examined our tendency to overextend ourselves by satisfying the demands and needs of others. Building boundaries according to God's wisdom frees us to live a Spirit-led life. Please take a few minutes to read or review the content from that chapter. In this study, we will deepen our understanding of godly boundaries by examining the Parable of the Ten Virgins.

The Lie: I can do it all if I just work harder.

Self-Driven Stronghold: I will ignore my personal needs and boundaries so I can serve others.

As soon as I heard her voice, I regretted accepting the call. I'd only known her for a few months, but during that time she bounced from one crisis to another. Each time she called and asked for my help, I found it hard to refuse. "How tiring it must be," I thought, "to have to face so many difficult situations."

But as time progressed, I was the exhausted one. One week she needed help cleaning her house for some unexpected guests. A few days later she asked me to watch her children while she went to an emergency dental appointment. When her car broke down, she needed me to run errands for her. Always a bargain hunter, she couldn't resist a sale. After overspending, she needed to borrow money until payday. During flu season she missed several days of work and then needed help catching up on her assignments. I already had a full schedule with my work assignments and family responsibilities. But because each need came wrapped up as an emergency, I felt it necessary to drop my plans and come to her rescue.

In true emergencies, I believe most people naturally want to help. As self-driven achievers, this desire to help others can be further fueled by our desire to people-please, or our tendency to build our worth through our achievements. We find it difficult to discern a true emergency from irresponsibility, so we quickly jump in to help—piling more on our already full plate. But when we continually overextend ourselves, we risk our health and well-being.

How do you respond when someone asks you for help? What prompts you to agree?

....

....

....

....

....

....

....

....

....

....

....

Day Two: The Ten Virgins—Accepting Their Responsibilities

During His ministry, Jesus often used the customs of Jewish marriages to portray the relationship between God and the church. His teaching in "The Parable of the Ten Virgins" is one example of this illustration.

✎ Read and Note

The entire parable is found in Matthew 25:1–13. In this study, we will examine the parable in sections.

When we think of Jesus as the groom and the church as His bride, we can see this parable refers to His coming. It clearly teaches we need to be ready for when Jesus returns.

Now let's look at what the parable can teach us about building boundaries.

Read Matthew 25:1–5.

In Jesus' culture weddings were celebrated as a community. After a couple entered into a contract to be married, the groom returned to his father's homestead to build a home for his bride. During this time, the bride continued to live with her family and prepared for her wedding and new home. This period of time generally lasted about a year.

When their new home was ready, the groom received his father's permission to collect his bride. The groom's party announced his arrival by shouting and blowing a trumpet. At that point, the entire community gathered in a procession leading to the couple's new home. The bridesmaids had the responsibility to light the path for the procession.

Since only the groom's father knew the timing of his son's return, the bride and her attendants needed to stay in a state of readiness. Both she and her bridesmaids had their lamps ready to be lit. To make sure their lamps could last until they arrived at their destination, they kept an extra supply of oil.

There are ten bridesmaids divided into two groups. How are each of the two groups described?

....

....

....

....

....

....

....

Each bridesmaid accepted the responsibility to light the way for the bridal procession. In the chapter in the book, we looked at the difference between a load and a burden. Would the responsibility of the bridesmaids be a load or a burden?

....

....

....

....

....

....

....

....

What sets the wise bridesmaids apart from the foolish ones? (How did the two groups prepare for their responsibility?)

The Greek word used for *foolish* in verse two is *móros*.[1] It carries the connotation of being dull in understanding or not having a grip on reality. How does this word explain why they didn't bring extra oil?

The Greek word for *wise* in verse two is *phronimos*.[2] It can also be translated as sensible or prudent. In what ways do the wise bridesmaids fit this description?

Look at verse 5. What problem did the bridesmaids face? Could it have been foreseen?

....

....

....

....

What do the bridesmaids do as they wait for the groom? What could the foolish ones have done instead?

....

....

....

....

Here is a gem of wisdom about planning, "The plans of the diligent lead to profit, as surely as haste leads to poverty" (Proverbs 21:5). What is the natural result of planning diligently?

....

....

....

....

What is the natural consequence of being too hasty and not planning properly?

....

....

....

....

....

Day Three: The Ten Virgins—Accepting Their Responsibilities

💬 Reflect and Apply

Think about your work habits. In what ways can you relate to the wise bridesmaids?

In what ways can you relate to the foolish bridesmaids?

Describe a time when you felt unprepared for a responsibility.

....

....

....

....

....

How did your lack of preparation make you feel? What did you learn from the experience?

....

....

....

....

....

On the other end of the spectrum is the tendency to be overprepared. This can cause us to overextend ourselves or to overspend our resources. Describe a time when you've been overprepared for a task. What did you learn from the experience?

....

....

....

....

....

Day Four: The Ten Virgins—Fulfilling Their Responsibilities

✎ Read and Note

Read Matthew 25:6–12.

When the bridegroom arrives at midnight, what request do the foolish bridesmaids make? Do the wise bridesmaids agree to their request?

....

....

....

....

....

Think about the wise ones and their refusal to help the foolish ones. Would you have used a different adjective to describe them?

....

....

....

....

....

For many years I struggled with this particular parable. When I read it, I saw the wise bridesmaids as selfish. Why wouldn't they be willing to share their provision of oil? It always troubled me that Jesus never called them selfish, only wise.

But as we learn to build boundaries, we can see another layer to the wisdom of these bridesmaids. They built and maintained healthy boundaries. Let's look at how they did this.

Reread verse 9. Why did the wise bridesmaids refuse to share their oil? What does this say about their level of preparation?

....

....

....

....

We have all heard the saying, "Your lack of planning is not my emergency." How does this statement apply to the situation with the bridesmaids?

....

....

....

....

The wise bridesmaids brought just the right amount of oil to meet their responsibilities. They didn't overspend and bring too much. And they didn't bring too little. How does this show wisdom?

....

....

....

....

The wise bridesmaids didn't just refuse to share their oil, they also offered something else. What was it?

....

....

....

....

The suggestion they offered could have worked. Even though it was the middle of the night, the community would be gathering to form the bridal procession. Somewhere among the participants, the foolish bridesmaids could find some oil to buy. But what happened when they left to buy more oil?

....

....

....

....

....

How did the wise bridesmaids model boundaries?

....

....

....

....

....

What happened to the foolish ones? What could they learn from this experience?

....

....

....

....

....

....

....

Would they have learned the lesson if the wise bridesmaids had not protected their boundaries?

....

....

....

....

....

....

....

....

Day Five: The Ten Virgins—Fulfilling Their Responsibilities

💬 Reflect and Apply

Have there been times when someone else's lack of planning impacted you? How did you respond?

....

....

....

....

....

....

Imagine yourself as one of the wise bridesmaids. What would you have done?

....

....

....

....

....

....

....

If I had been one of these bridesmaids (before I learned the value of boundaries), my story would have ended in one of two ways. After buying way too much oil and lugging it with me throughout the procession, I would have walked into the wedding banquet too exhausted to enjoy myself. Or I would have given away my oil and rushed off to buy more in the market. Arriving too late, I would have completely missed out on the festivities.

What are some of the negative consequences you've suffered because you assumed someone else's responsibility, or rescued someone from their poor planning?

....

....

....

....

How would you handle these situations differently by setting godly boundaries?

....

....

....

....

Where in your life do you think you're doing a good job with healthy boundaries? Where do you need to build them?

....

....

....

....

Day Six: Conclusion

Truth: God established boundaries to protect us from doing too much.

Spirit-Led Conviction: I will build boundaries and trust meeting this God-given need will protect my overall well-being.

⊘ Resolve to Take Action

As we wrap up our study on building boundaries, take some time to sit with the Holy Spirit. Ask Him to help you answer the following questions:

In the book, we discussed learning to say "no" and establishing boundaries. These will help us get the rest we need as well as free us to choose projects and activities that align with our gifts and skill set. How different would your life look if you established these boundaries where you need them?

....

....

....

....

What stands in your way of building these boundaries? What can you do to overcome the obstacles?

....

....

....

....

....

Write out a personal statement of commitment to help you stay true to your boundaries. For example:

- I will stop rescuing people from their lack of planning and trust they will learn from their mistakes.

- I will obey God's commands to rest from my work.

....

....

....

....

....

....

Write out a prayer to God. Share with Him your plans to build and maintain boundaries. Ask Him to help you implement it.

....

....

....

....

....

....

....

....

CHAPTER 7

Easing Expectations

Day One: Introduction

In chapter seven of the book, we explored our inclination to assume unrealistic expectations. Frustration over meeting these expectations can cause us to treat ourselves or others harshly. In the process, we develop a highly critical and unkind inner voice. Please take some time to read or reflect on the information in that chapter. In this study, we will learn how to tame the harshness created by unrealistic expectations and how to set realistic ones. Our text for this study will be the Parable of the Unmerciful Servant.

The Lie: No expectation is unreasonable.

Self-Driven Stronghold: I will push myself relentlessly and meet every expectation.

Looking up at the clock, I sighed in frustration. I'd already spent an hour on the assignment but had only completed a few of the problems. Math was my favorite subject, and I actually enjoyed solving complicated equations. Still, this assignment seemed unusually long.

Another hour went by. Although I worked steadily, I still had more problems to complete. Grumbling the whole time, I finally completed the assignment. It took over three hours, which meant sacrificing my other plans for the evening.

When I arrived in class the next morning, other students had approached the professor's desk. After speaking with them, he apologized to the class. Our professor had no idea how long the assignment would take, so he gave everyone extra time to finish it. All around me, the other students cheered. But I sat fuming in anger. If I could get it done, why couldn't they? I had never once considered not doing the assignment due to its unreasonable length.

My frustration that day had several layers. To complete the obnoxiously long assignment, I sacrificed my time and personal plans. I was the only one who did so, but the professor gave me no special recognition. And no one suffered any consequences for not completing the assignment. The whole situation felt unfair.

Unrealistic expectations come to us in many different ways, but we don't always recognize them as unreasonable. In my situation, I only realized the assignment was unreasonable when my classmates refused to do it. How do you determine if an expectation is unreasonable?

Day Two: Unmerciful Servant Receives Mercy

Jesus told this parable in response to a question from Peter about forgiveness. In His answer, Jesus implied we should be willing to forgive without limits. Jesus then used this parable to illustrate His point. As we study this parable, we will unpack its meaning using the lens of unrealistic expectations.

✎ Read and Note

Read Matthew 18:23–27.

The parable describes a king (or master) who settles the accounts of his servants. Look at the first servant he called.

How much money did this servant owe?

....

....

....

....

In the Greek translation, ten thousand bags of gold corresponded to ten thousand talents.[1]

When you consider that one talent equaled approximately twenty years of salary, how many years would it take for the servant to repay the king (10,000 x 20)? How realistic is it for the servant to repay the debt?

....

....

....

....

What recourse did the master plan to take in order to be repaid? How would you describe this plan? Reasonable? Harsh?

....

....

....

....

What is the servant's response to the master's plan? Does this surprise you? Would you have asked for something different?

....

....

....

....

Rather than asking for a reduction in the debt owed, the servant asked for more time to repay it. What does this reveal about his understanding of the debt he owed and his resources to pay it?

....

....

....

....

....

The servant might be underestimating what it will take for him to repay his debt. What could cause him to overlook these important details?

....

....

....

....

....

He also might be overestimating his ability to repay the debt. Why might he do this? (Think about his character and habits—especially in meeting the expectations of others.)

....

....

....

....

How does the master respond to the servant's request? How would you feel if you were the servant?

....

....

....

....

....

....

Day Three: The Unmerciful Servant Receives Mercy

💬 Reflect and Apply

Despite the staggering amount he owed, the servant promised to repay it *if he could have more time.* In what ways have you underestimated what an expectation would cost you in terms of your resources—especially of time and effort? What can help you avoid this trap?

....

....

....

....

Not only did the servant underestimate his resources, but he also overestimated his ability to pay the debt. In what ways have you overestimated your ability to meet an expectation? How can you stop yourself from doing this?

....

....

....

....

Think about some of the current expectations you are trying to meet. Take an honest inventory of your available resources, especially of time. Are any of these unrealistic for you?

....

....

....

Who has this expectation of you? In the book, we discussed negotiating for more reasonable expectations. How can you do this in these cases?

....

....

....

....

....

....

....

Look back at the section "Learning How to Set Realistic Expectations" in chapter seven of the book. What are some practical steps you can take to prevent accepting unrealistic expectations in the future?

....

....

....

....

....

....

....

Day Four: The Unmerciful Servant Rejects Mercy

✎ Read and Note

Read Matthew 18:26–34.

The master completely forgave the servant's staggering debt. How did the servant respond?

....

....

....

....

....

....

The unmerciful servant began trying to repay his debt by calling in the money others owed him. How much did his fellow servant owe?

....

....

....

....

....

In the Greek translation, these one hundred silver coins corresponded to one hundred denarii.[2]

Laborers received one denarius for each day's work. How many days would it take for this servant to pay his debt (1 x 100)? Approximately how many months? How realistic would it be for him to repay?

....

....

....

....

What did the fellow servant ask? Does this seem like a reasonable request?

....

....

....

....

How did the unmerciful servant respond?

....

....

....

....

In Jesus' culture, people expected those who were forgiven of a debt to also forgive those who owed them money.[3] Why would the unmerciful servant not honor this cultural expectation (look back at verse 26)?

....

....

....

....

Reread verse 31.

Who noticed the harshness of the unmerciful servant?

....

....

What did they do in response?

....

....

What was the outcome for the unmerciful servant?

....

....

What does this show us about the cycle of harshness?

....

....

Day Five: The Unmerciful Servant Rejects Mercy

💬 Reflect and Apply

The unmerciful servant rejected the debt forgiveness of the master. Instead, he assumed the unrealistic expectation to pay his debt. In the book, we discussed the need to show ourselves the same compassion as God does. In what ways do you reject His compassion and try to meet unrealistic expectations?

....

....

....

....

....

The unmerciful servant called in the debt of his fellow servant. We see him pulling together all his resources as he tries to pay his debt. In what ways do you expend all your available resources to meet an unrealistic expectation?

....

....

....

....

....

The unmerciful servant became frustrated when his fellow servant couldn't pay his debt. His frustration spilled out in harshness. In what ways does frustration over unrealistic expectations create callousness in your life?

....

....

....

....

....

The unmerciful servant didn't see anything wrong with how he treated his fellow servant. In what ways are you blinded to how unrealistic expectations affect you? How have other people pointed out your impatience, or commented on how hard you are on yourself?

....

....

....

....

What steps do you need to take for you to accept God's compassion?

....

....

....

....

Day Six: Conclusion

Truth: God has only reasonable expectations of us.

Spirit-Led Conviction: I will ease the expectations I place on myself and make them reasonable.

⊘ Resolve to Take Action

When the master forgave his debt, he gave the unmerciful servant the freedom to end his cycle of harshness. Unfortunately, he refused to let go of his unrealistic resolve to pay his debt. By refusing to accept his master's compassion, he never freed himself of it.

As we wrap up our study on harshness, take time to sit with the Holy Spirit and reflect on the following questions:

Describe how different your days would look if you accepted God's compassion and eased the unrealistic expectations in your life.

....

....

....

....

....

....

....

....

What obstacles do you face in trying to lessen your expectations? How will you overcome these?

_____

_____

_____

_____

_____

_____

Write out a personal statement of commitment to help you overcome harshness. For example:

- I will learn to accept the compassion God has for me so I won't accept unrealistic expectations.

- I will practice the spiritual disciplines of solitude and silence so I can transform the harshness of my inner voice.

Write out a prayer to God asking Him to help you accept His compassion so you can ease the expectations.

_____

_____

_____

_____

_____

CHAPTER 8

Cultivating
Collaboration

Day One: Introduction

In chapter eight in the book, we examined our reluctance to work with others and our desire to stay independent and self-reliant. We learned that God created us to collaborate with others and that we will reap benefits when we do. Please take some time to read or review the information from that chapter. In this study, we will learn how conflict resolution is part of the collaborative process.

The Lie: I can only trust myself.

Self-Driven Stronghold: I will work harder in the group to make sure we succeed.

Despite the cheerful decor in the classroom, the tension among the women seated at the table created an unwelcome vibe. I took my seat and prayed for wisdom and diplomacy. These four teachers met weekly to make decisions for the students in their care. Three of them had worked together previously. The fourth teacher, new to our school and district, had transferred from another state. As an experienced teacher, she held strong opinions and never shied away from voicing them. Her forceful personality clashed with the equally strong lead teacher. Because this group had struggled to work together productively, I, as an Instructional Coach, had been invited to their meetings to facilitate their work together.

As the team began discussing that day's agenda items, the new teacher interrupted the conversation. Looking directly at the lead teacher she launched an accusation, "You are a bully. We all have to agree with what you want to do. The rest of us have no voice on this team."

In the stunned silence that followed, I watched as each team member's eyes bounced from the new teacher to the lead teacher, and then to me. Taking a deep breath, I entered the fray and addressed the new teacher. "Do you have a specific example of this? Because last week I remember the lead teacher yielded to your position regarding the writing assignment."

The new teacher looked at me, thought for a moment, and then answered, "No, I don't. But it doesn't matter. I'm resigning today." With that, she stood up, and strode regally out of the room, down the hall, and into our principal's office. There she made good on her word and promptly resigned.

The rest of us stared at each other as we struggled to process what had just happened. I never could have envisioned this outcome of the meeting.

In the following weeks, the remaining three teachers forged a new unity and became a strong collaborative team. Through this experience, we learned some people will refuse to collaborate with us, no matter how hard we try. But this is very rare. In most cases, conflicts can be resolved as part of the process.

What types of conflicts have you experienced when working with others?

....

....

....

....

....

Day Two: The Dispute over the Gentile Believers

✎ Read and Note

The early church was unified in its goal to evangelize the world. Despite their diverse ethnicities and personalities, they worked together to spread the Gospel. But that doesn't mean they didn't experience conflict. Let's look at one of these situations from the book of Acts.

Read Acts 15:1–5.

In the earliest days of the church, the members were mostly Jews. But as the Gospel continued to spread, more Gentiles became Christians.

As part of their missionary work, Paul and Barnabas had been working with the church in Antioch for some time. The members of the church consisted mostly of Gentile Christians.

In this passage, we see the arrival of some people from Judea. What do they begin to teach the believers?

_____

_____

_____

_____

_____

Circumcision was the physical sign of God's Old Testament covenant with the Jewish people. That covenant also had many other commandments which they referred to as the law of Moses. Circumcision set the Jewish people apart and identified them as God's chosen people.

What would be the significance of asking the Gentile Christians to be circumcised?

....

....

....

The conflict between the two groups raised the question: Do Gentiles need to become Jews (through circumcision) before becoming Christians?

How did Paul and Barnabas react?

....

....

....

....

....

At this point many Gentiles had been converted throughout the Roman empire. What impact could this teaching have on the universal church?

....

....

....

....

....

What did they decide to do to resolve this conflict?

Who would be included in the collaboration?

As they traveled to Jerusalem, what did they share with the Christians in Phoenicia and Samaria? How did they respond to the news?

Once they arrived in Jerusalem, what did they do?

Once again, we see the Gentile issue raised. Which group raised the issue?

The Pharisees were strict followers of the law of Moses. Some of them had been converted to Christianity, but they maintained their observation of the law. In addition to being circumcised, they added another requirement for the Gentiles. What was it?

....

....

....

....

....

....

....

Day Three: The Dispute over the Gentile Believers

💬 Reflect and Apply

Imagine the scene. In the group, you have people who feel adamantly that Gentiles should follow the law of Moses. You have another group who feels just as strongly that this should not be required of them. These types of strong, passionate disagreements are common when people work together.

What challenges do you face when working with people who strongly disagree?

....

....

....

....

....

Think of a time when you worked with people who passionately debated a course of action. How was it resolved? Did the disagreement break down collaboration?

....

....

....

....

....

Look back at the section "Leaning on God's Wisdom When Collaboration Breaks Down" in chapter eight of the book. What are some ways God advises us to respond when we disagree with others? How can these responses promote healthy and productive conflict?

....

....

....

....

We read in Proverbs 27:17, "As iron sharpens iron, so one person sharpens another." In what ways have you grown sharper through the process of collaboration?

....

....

....

....

....

The believers had to travel to meet with the council in Jerusalem which could have been inconvenient. In what ways can working with others be an inconvenience?

....

....

....

....

....

Day Four: The Council in Jerusalem Resolves the Issue

✎ Read and Note

Let's continue reading the collaboration account.

Read Acts 15: 6–12.

After the party of Pharisees shared their convictions, what did the apostles and elders decide to do?

....

....

Next, the apostle Peter stood up to address the council. What was his position on the issue (v.10–11)?

....

....

What reason does he give for his stance (v. 8–9)?

....

....

The council then listened to Paul and Barnabas. How did they explain their conviction (v.12)?

....

....

....

133

Now read Acts 15:13–20.

Finally, James, the brother of Jesus, gave his assessment. In his response, he referred to an Old Testament prophecy that reveals God's promise to be the Lord of all who seek Him. God specifically refers to a group of people by name. Who are they (v.17)? What would be the significance of this detail?

....

....

....

....

....

Because the prophecy specifically names the Gentiles, James concluded they didn't have to become Jews (v.19). However, he suggested asking the Gentiles to abstain from certain things. What were they?

....

....

....

....

....

The four things listed were all part of pagan idol worship, which was prevalent in the Gentile culture. James suggested asking the Gentile Christians to no longer participate. However, as Christians, they would be expected to follow the teachings of Jesus.

Read Acts 15:23–29.

What was the council's decision?

How was the council's decision communicated?

Each of these members of the group brought their unique perspectives and experiences to the collaboration process. How did that help them to come to a resolution?

A consensus happens when all members of a group agree to a course of action. This is not the same as casting votes and going with the majority opinion. In those cases, some members are outvoted and forced to follow the plan of the majority. In true collaboration, everyone works together until they agree to follow the same plan.

How can we see that the council reached a consensus through collaboration?

Day Five: The Council in Jerusalem Resolves the Issue

💬 Reflect and Apply

How can the different perspectives and experiences of others help us reach a better solution to a problem?

....

....

....

How easy has it been for you to reach an agreement when working with others? What has made it challenging?

....

....

....

....

Have you ever been in a situation where you held the minority opinion and were outvoted? How did it feel to be forced to follow that plan?

....

....

....

....

Instead of voting and letting the majority rule, teams can continue working together until they reach a consensus. In this case, the plan is ironed out until everyone can agree to it. How would that be a better model of collaboration?

....

....

....

....

....

....

....

How has your attitude about collaboration changed?

....

....

....

....

....

....

....

....

Day Six: Conclusion

Truth: God established collaboration as the means for us to do our best work.

Spirit-Led Conviction: I will embrace collaboration as God intended.

⊘ Resolve to Take Action

As we wrap up this week's study, take time to sit with the Holy Spirit. Ask Him to help you discern the answers to the following questions:

How different would your life look if you embraced God's plan for collaboration?

....

....

....

....

....

What steps do you need to take to embrace collaboration? What could stand in your way?

....

....

....

....

....

Write out a personal statement of commitment to help you take these steps. For example:

- I will trust God's plan for collaboration, even when I don't see the benefits.

- I will do my best to work with others to reach a common goal.

....

....

....

....

....

....

....

Write out a prayer to God where you commit to the process of collaboration. Ask Him to help you work through any resistance you still have.

....

....

....

....

....

....

....

CHAPTER 9

Letting The Spirit Lead

Day One: Introduction

In chapter nine of the book, we discussed ways to continue our partnership with the Holy Spirit. Please take some time to read or review the content from that chapter. In this study, we will deepen our understanding of how the Spirit works in our lives.

Spirit-Led Conviction: I will keep in step with the Spirit.

Right there, in the middle of the dining room of the fast-food restaurant, tears began streaming down my face. I'd stopped in for a quick bite before heading to the evening service of my church. I'd only been a Christian for a few months, but already felt disillusioned. I thought following Jesus rather than the world would make my life simpler and more fulfilling. Instead, I felt as if I were crumbling under the weight of trying to balance my new life with the demands of my university studies and other responsibilities.

Hoping to find some comfort in God's Word, I opened my Bible to the Gospel of Matthew. But the passage I read that afternoon unleashed a stream of pent-up tears:

> "Come to me, all you who are weary and burdened, and I will give you rest. Take my yoke upon you and learn from me, for I am gentle and humble in heart, and you will find rest for your souls. For my yoke is easy and my burden is light." Matthew 11:28–30

"Jesus," I sobbed. "I don't know what is wrong. But Your yoke does not feel easy, and Your burden does not feel light."

That was over forty years ago. I wish I could say that was the last time following Jesus felt like a burden. Many times, I returned to this passage and asked for clarity. "Why can't I get it together, so my Christian walk feels easy and light?"

Jesus originally spoke these words to the Jews who felt the burden of trying to follow both the written law and the oral traditions created by the Pharisees. Jesus referred to these additional requirements as "heavy, cumbersome loads" (Matthew 23:4).

Although we aren't expected to follow the law or the traditions, we are called to imitate Jesus who lived a perfect life. For any of us, this is a high calling. But it is even more stressful for self-driven people like me. Instinctively I knew my struggle came from relying on myself rather than on God. But I also didn't know how to tap into the power of the Holy Spirit. So my life became a pattern of holding myself back from what's wrong and pushing myself forward to do what's right. No wonder I felt burdened and weary!

In what ways has your Christian walk felt heavy and burdensome?

....

....

....

....

....

....

....

....

Day Two: Jesus Modeled the Spiritual Disciplines

Throughout the book, we practiced spiritual disciplines to help us tap into the power of the Holy Spirit. In today's study, we will look at how Jesus modeled some of these practices.

✎ Read and Note

Read Luke 5:15–16.

Describe what is happening at this time in Jesus' ministry.

....

....

....

....

....

....

How does the Bible describe the number of people who are looking for Jesus? What picture does this give you?

....

....

....

....

....

....

What did Jesus do in response to the pressures He felt?

....

....

....

....

In these verses, Jesus modeled the spiritual practices of solitude and silence. In the book, we used these practices to help us connect with the Holy Spirit and His transformative power.

What distractions did Jesus face? How could the practice of solitude help Him?

....

....

....

....

Read John 8:29. In this verse, Jesus describes His relationship with His Father. What claim did He make?

....

....

....

....

....

How could Jesus be sure of what would please God? (Look back at Luke 5:16.)

....

....

....

....

....

....

There are many different forms of prayer. In the book, we often practiced the prayer of silence as a means of surrendering our self-driven ways to the will of God.

The Bible doesn't reveal the words of Jesus' prayers during His times of solitude. But what can we conclude based on the claim He made?

....

....

Read John 12:49–50. What claim does Jesus make here?

....

....

....

....

....

What type of prayer would help Him know what God wanted Him to say?

....

....

....

How did the spiritual practices of solitude and silence prepare Jesus for His daily ministry?

....

....

....

....

....

....

....

Day Three: Jesus Modeled the Spiritual Disciplines

💬 Reflect and Apply

What are some of the distractions you face on a regular basis? These can be thoughts, attitudes, concerns, activities, people—anything that keeps you from feeling connected to Jesus and the plan He has for your life.

How can the spiritual discipline of solitude help you?

....

....

....

....

In the Lord's prayer, Jesus taught us to pray for God's will to be done on earth (Matthew 6:9-10). How might this prayer apply to you?

....

....

....

....

What challenges do you face as you try to surrender your will so God's will can be done?

....

....

....

How can the spiritual discipline of silence help you?

....

....

....

....

....

....

....

....

Day Four: Redirecting the Apostle Paul

One of our biggest obstacles to seeking direction from the Holy Spirit is our fear of hearing Him incorrectly. To help us overcome this fear, let's look at the life of the apostle Paul.

✎ Read and Note

Read Acts 23:1.

This hearing before the Sanhedrin happened near the end of Paul's life. What amazing claim did Paul make?

....

....

....

....

....

We know Paul originally persecuted Christians. In our first week of study, we uncovered how he could do this and think it was God's will. As a reminder, read John 16:2. What lie did Paul believe?

....

....

....

....

....

Paul thought he was listening to God's voice, but he was mistaken. In his heart Paul always wanted to serve God. So God intervened.

Read Acts 9:3–6.

How did God redirect Paul?

....

....

....

After his conversion, Paul continued to be zealous for God. This time his zeal pushed him to preach the Gospel. The Lord led Paul to travel as a missionary.

Let's look at how the Spirit directed, and then redirected, his steps during his second missionary trip.

Read Acts 16:6–12.

Paul wanted to preach in the province of Asia. Who stopped him?

....

....

Where did Paul want to go next (v. 7). What kept them from going there?

....

....

Where did they go next (v. 8)?

....

....

How did Paul know where he should go next (v. 9)?

....

....

....

Paul and his companions concluded that God called them to preach the Gospel in Macedonia. Where did they eventually land?

....

....

....

Read Acts 16:13–15.

Philippi did not have a synagogue, probably because there were very few Jewish people living there. Instead, the Jewish people would gather together near a river. So on the Sabbath, Paul went to the river to find a place to pray, and to meet up with other Jews.

Paul shared the Gospel with the people who had gathered there. In the vision Paul received, he saw a man asking for help. But who actually responded to Paul's message? How is this different from the vision he had received?

....

....

....

....

....

In these passages, we see how Paul was continually redirected. After pivoting him from a lie to the truth, the Spirit continued to move in his life. He rerouted him to the cities where Paul was meant to preach. The Spirit even showed Paul that different people would respond to the Gospel (women instead of men).

How did Paul respond to all of these redirections? Did he get stubborn or bitter? What helped him be at peace through all the changes?

Day Five: Redirecting the Apostle Paul

💬 Reflect and Apply

Paul continuously sought the Lord's will. Sometimes he got it wrong so God corrected him. Can you think of some situations where God redirected you from the path you were on?

....

....

....

....

How do you feel about these course corrections?

....

....

The law of physics tells us it takes less energy to turn a ship around than to get it moving from a standstill. What does this mean for you as you consider stepping out on faith? Will it be harder for God to redirect you, or to get you to take that step?

....

....

....

....

....

In the book, we discussed how the Spirit will never ask us to do something that violates God's commands. That still leaves a big gray area where we are left to choose between what is good and what is best. How can Paul's life resolve your fear of making the wrong choice or hearing the wrong voice?

....

....

....

....

....

....

Paul's heart always wanted to do God's will, and this is what allowed him to be so easily redirected. How can you use the spiritual practices of solitude and silence to help you cultivate a heart of surrender?

....

....

....

....

....

....

....

Day Six: Conclusion

Truth: God gave us His Spirit to help us.

Spirit-Led Conviction: I will keep in step with the Spirit.

As we wrap up our study this week, please take some time to sit with the Holy Spirit and process the following questions.

⊘ Resolve to Take Action

How would your life look if you engaged in the spiritual practices of solitude and silence on a regular basis? How would these disciplines help you to surrender your will so that God's will can be done in your life?

....

....

....

....

....

What resistance do you have to partner with the Holy Spirit? How can you resolve these reservations so you can step out in faith?

....

....

....

....

....

Write out a statement of commitment to help you in your journey to be led by the Spirit. For example:

- I will engage in the spiritual practices of solitude and silence and learn to listen to the Spirit's guidance.

- I will step out in faith and trust God will redirect me when necessary.

Write out a prayer to help you trust God and the help He sends through His Holy Spirit.

Acknowledgments

"Every good and perfect gift is from above,
coming down from the Father of the heavenly lights."

James 1:17a

Writing, the actual process of putting words on a page, is a solitary endeavor. But it takes a community to take those pages, publish them, and make them known to readers. I have so many to thank.

First of all, I'm so grateful for my husband, Mark, who has given me the time, space, and resources to pursue this dream. He not only supported me as I wrote this book, but he also walked beside me as I experienced many of the lessons I share in its pages. Thank you for your midnight runs to the post office on those crazy April 15 nights, for helping me set up (and take down) my classroom each year, and for listening to my early writing drafts. Your steadfast nature perfectly balances my self-driven achiever personality. I'm so thankful I could lean on your calming strength through all of life's ups and downs. You truly are my better half. We're still having fun, and you're still the one!

Next, a huge thank you to my children: Kendra, Daniel, and Katia. I've learned so much from being your mom. Because of you I finally understood what it means to love unconditionally. I love you all to the moon and back, and then some. Thank you for filling my life with joy. I love the adults you have become (even if I still miss the time when you were kids). Keep following your passions and loving life—you inspire me!

Kudos to Buddy, my father-in-law, who allowed us to turn his life and house inside out and upside down when we moved to Virginia. Thank you for cheering me on in my writing projects.

A big shout out to my two close friends: Jody Rohleder and Teresa Linner. These two women have been by my side for many of the experiences noted in this book. Thank you for helping me keep a spiritual perspective and finding strength in God during the tough times. You believed in me when I didn't believe in myself. Without you and your friendship, this book would not have been written.

I am deeply indebted to Benjamin and Melina Hutchins who trained me in the spiritual disciplines. Because of your training, I learned how to access the transformative power of the Holy Spirit. I will be forever grateful to both of you.

The community at COMPEL Training will always have a special place in my heart. I would never have become a writer if not for this incredible ministry. I'm grateful for the insightful training, publishing opportunities, friends, and support you have given me. You helped me find and then refine my writing voice.

Mindy Kiker and Jennifer Kochert and the Flourish Academy Community—thank you! Your practical classes and coaching calls provided the necessary steps to organize and publish this book. I can't thank you enough for the invaluable counsel you provide.

Many thanks to my COMPEL Critique Group members—Margaret, Carmella, Joy, Linda (1), Rachel, Linda (2), Michelle, and Joanna. Your critiques make me a stronger writer. Thank you for lending your insights and wisdom to several chapters of this book. I value your input, both as writers and as fellow teachers of God's Word.

For my first ever focus group: Allie, Briana, Cat, Jeannette, Jenni, Jody, Kat, Kendra, Margaret, Sarah, Sheila, Shelby, Tabitha, and Teresa: a thousand thanks for partnering with me on this book project! Having you on board kept me motivated and on track. Your feedback provided the information I needed to make sure this book would meet people's needs. You exhibited collaboration at its best. Thank you!

I'm so appreciative for Melanie Chitwood who edited the first edition of this book. From the very beginning you expressed a desire to make this book the best it could be. Thank you for praying over this book and for our partnership.

Through a number of events, the Holy Spirit led me to work with Mandy Roberson and the team at Market Refined Media & Publishing. They have truly been instrumental in bringing this second edition to life. I appreciate their wisdom, integrity, and professionalism. I'm so blessed to work with such an incredible group of people.

A huge component of the MRM team is Carey Scott who edited this second edition. I love your insights, encouragement, and constructive criticisms. You not only made this book better; you helped me grow as a writer. Thank you for sharing your expertise with me!

Of course, none of this would be possible without the saving grace of Jesus. Over forty years ago, God sent a Christian and professional woman, Nancy, into my workplace. Her exemplary life became the first Bible I ever read. Her unwavering joy attracted me to her church, and ultimately to Jesus. She taught me the importance of modeling Jesus in our workplaces. I will be eternally grateful for her friendship.

Finally, I thank you, my readers. Of all the books available, you chose to spend your time and energy on this one. I am grateful for your readership and pray the lessons He taught me will bless your life as well.

God never ceases to amaze me with His good and perfect gifts.

About the Author

Prompted by gratitude, Shirley Desmond Jackson loves to teach others the truths found in God's Word. Her driving passion is to help women connect with an extraordinary God who meets us in the middle of our ordinary lives. After serving on the foreign mission field in Paris, France, she married her best friend, Mark. Together they raised three children and now shepherd the Married Ministry of their church. In her free time, she loves to spend time with family—especially her two precious grandchildren.

For more Bible lessons and materials, connect with Shirley on her website at shirleydesmondjackson.com. You can also find her on Facebook and Instagram.

Endnotes

Chapter 1

1   Vocabulary.com, s.v. "good-enough (adj)," accessed March 29, 2022, https://www.vocabulary.com/dictionary/good%20enough#:~:text=adjective,suitable%20for%20a%20thing%20specified

2   Biblehub.com, s.v., "banah (v)," accessed June 8, 2024, https://biblehub.com/hebrew/1129.htm

3   Dictionary.com, s.v., "fashion (v)," accessed June 8, 2024, https://www.dictionary.com/browse/fashion

4   Biblehub.com, s.v. "poiéma (n)," accessed April 17, 2022, https://biblehub.com/greek/4161.htm

5   "What does Philippians 3:5 mean?," Bible Ref, accessed February 4, 2022, https://www.bibleref.com/Philippians/3/Philippians-3-5.html

6   Richard Niell Donovan, "Biblical Commentary (Bible Study) Philippians 3:4b–14," Sermon Writer, accessed February 4, 2022, https://sermonwriter.com/biblical-commentary-old/philippians-34b-14/

7   Ibid.

Chapter 2

1   "What does Mark 5:25 mean?," Bible Ref, accessed April 18, 2022, https://www.bibleref.com/Mark/5/Mark-5-25.html

Chapter 4

1   Martin Charlesworth, "The Parable of the Ten 'Minas,'" The Life of Jesus-Series 10: Episode 12, July 30, 2020, https://wordonline.org/videos/the-parable-of-the-ten-minas?lang=en

2   NIV Cultural Backgrounds Study Bible, (China: Zondervan, 2016), 1787–1788

Chapter 5

1   Carlos Barquero, "57% if Gen Zers want to be influencers—but 'it's constant, Monday through Sunday,' says creator," CNBC make it, accessed October 7, 2024, https://www.cnbc.com/2024/09/14/more-than-half-of-gen-z-want-to-be-influencers-but-its-constant.html#:~:text=More%20than%20half%20of%20young,survey%20of%202%2C204%20U.S.%20adults.

2   Merriam-webster.com, s.v., "influencer (n)," accessed June 22, 2024, https://www.merriam-webster.com/dictionary/influencer

3   Jacinda Santora, "12 Types of Influencers You Can Use to Improve Your Marketing," Influencer Marketing Hub, accessed June 23, 2024, https://influencermarketinghub.com/types-of-influencers/

4   "Status of Global Christianity, 2021, in the Context of 1900–2050," Gordon Conwell Theology, accessed October 7, 2021, https://www.gordonconwell.edu/center-for-global-christianity/wp-content/uploads/sites/13/2020/12/Status-of-Global-Christianity-2021.pdf

5   "What can we learn from Jesus' feeding of the 5,000?," Got Questions, accessed October 7, 2021, https://www.gotquestions.org/feeding-the-5000.html

6   "Who were the Pharisees?," Got Questions, accessed October 7, 2021, https://www.gotquestions.org/Pharisees.html

7   Evelyn and Frank Stagg, "Jesus and Women" Christianity Today, accessed October 7, 2021, https://www.christianitytoday.com/history/issues/issue-17/jesus-and-women.html

8   "What can we learn from what the Bible says about Jesus and women?," Got Questions, accessed October 7, 2021, https://www.gotquestions.org/Jesus-and-women.html

9   Richard Niell Donovan, "Biblical Commentary (Bible Study) John 4:5–42," Sermon Writer, accessed October 7, 2021, https://sermonwriter.com/biblical-commentary-old/john-45-42/

10   Richard Niell Donovan, "Biblical Commentary (Bible Study) Luke 10:38–42, Sermon Writer, accessed October 7, 2021, https://sermonwriter.com/biblical-commentary-old/luke-1038-42/

11   "What is the significance of Jesus eating with sinners?," Got Questions, accessed October 7, 2021, https://www.gotquestions.org/Jesus-with-sinners.html

Chapter 6

1   Biblehub.com, s.v., "móros (adj.)," accessed July 7, 2024, https://biblehub.com/greek/3474.htm

2   Biblehub.com, s.v., phronimos (adj.)," accessed July 7, 2024, https://biblehub.com/greek/5429.htm

Chapter 7

1   Richard Niell Donovan, "Biblical Commentary (Bible Study) Matthew 18:21–35," Sermon Writer, accessed January 6, 2022, https://sermonwriter.com/biblical-commentary-old/matthew-1821-35/

2   Ibid.

3   Ibid.

Notes